POLITICAL ELITES
IN A DEMOCRACY

The Editor

PETER BACHRACH is Professor of Political
Science at Temple University. He received his
B.A. from Reed College and his Ph.D. from
Harvard University. Dr. Bachrach is a member
of the selection committee of the Woodrow Wilson Fellowship Foundation and Director of the
American Civil Liberties Union of Greater Philadelphia. He is the author of *Problem in Freedom*
and *The Theory of Democratic Elitism: A Critique,* and co-author of *Power and Poverty:
Theory and Practice.* In addition to numerous articles in scholarly publications, Dr. Bachrach has
contributed to several books in the field of political science, including "Corporate Authority and
Democratic Theory," an essay that appears in
Political Theory and Social Change, a volume
edited by David Spitz and published by Atherton
Press.

POLITICAL

EDITED BY

ELITES IN A DEMOCRACY

Peter Bachrach

ATHERTON PRESS

New York 1971

Political Elites in a Democracy
edited by Peter Bachrach

Address all inquiries to:
Atherton Press, Inc.
70 Fifth Avenue
New York 10011

Library of Congress Catalog Card Number 78–116534

FIRST EDITION

Manufactured in the United States of America
DESIGNED BY LORETTA LI

Contents

Introduction 1
PETER BACHRACH

1 : *The Elite Concept* 13
HAROLD D. LASSWELL, DANIEL LERNER,
  and C. EASTON ROTHWELL

2 : *Democratic Practice and Democratic Theory* 27
BERNARD BERELSON, PAUL LAZARSFELD,
  and WILLIAM MC PHEE

3 : *The American System in Crisis* 49
DAVID B. TRUMAN

4 : *A Critique of the Elitist Theory of
    Democracy* 69
JACK L. WALKER

5 : *Further Reflections on "The Elitist
    Theory of Democracy"* 93
ROBERT DAHL

6 : *The Case for Decentralization* 116
PAUL GOODMAN

7 : *Repressive Tolerance* 138
HERBERT MARCUSE

Index 171

Introduction

PETER BACHRACH

The meaning of the term political elites, the role such elites play in a free society, and their relationship to ordinary citizens have been recurring themes in the history of political thought since Plato's time. However, at this juncture in history these issues have assumed critical importance. The vast and growing disparity between the existence of the overwhelming predominance of elites in the decision-making process and the democratic ideal that each individual, to the greatest possible degree, should participate in making decisions that vitally affect him underlies these potentially explosive issues.

Referring to the fact that "key political, economic, and social decisions" are made by "tiny minorities," Robert Dahl concludes that "It is difficult—nay impossible—to see how it could be otherwise in large political systems."[1] It is also a fact, however, that a growing number of people among students and faculty within the university, among militant blacks and recipients of welfare within the ghetto, among the clergy and among intellectuals generally, refuse to accept the hard reality of elite rule. The forces of technology and bureaucracy that have sharply expanded the influence and the invisibility of elites have also created a profound reaction among nonelites. This reaction is reflected in demands for decentralization in decision-making and for widespread participation by nonelites at all levels of organized activity: within the political parties, in the local community, at work, at study, and at worship. It is no exaggeration to say that the problem of the place of political elites in democratic society is critical at this time.

I

Before reviewing the theoretical aspects of this problem, it is important to have a clear idea of the meaning and implications of the concept "political elite." Since Mosca's and Pareto's formulations of the concept at the turn of the century, most scholars conceive of political elites composed of individuals who actually exercise an inordinate amount of political power in society.[2] For example, Harold Lasswell defines the political elite "as the power holders of a body politic."[3] He further asserts that the "division into elite and mass is universal," and even in a republic, the "few exercise a relatively great weight of power, and the many exercise comparatively little."[4] Much can be said for this concept of an elite, but nevertheless it presents important difficulties and ambiguities.

First, it is unrealistic to conceive of elites solely in power terms. Indeed, elites wield power, but in most cases their resources of power reside in their occupation of a position of authority.[5] Moreover, the exercise of authority by elites is often more far-reaching and effective than when they merely choose to exercise power. The distinction between power and authority, which Lasswell blurs over,[6] is crucial. In the most simplistic terms, when power is exercised, compliance is forthcoming to avoid sanctions. An example would be a case where a man relinquished his wallet to an armed robber to avoid being shot. His wallet was of less value to him than his life, hence he complied with the demand of the power-wielder. Authority is exercised when obedience to a command results from either a belief in the legitimacy of the commander's position and his right to issue the order, or a feeling of loyalty and confidence in the sound judgment of the commander, or from both. The dramatic decline in the influence of President Lyndon Johnson inside and outside the country was not due to a lessening of his power resources or his will to exert power, but to the rapid deflation of his authority. More and more people began to regard his position on the Vietnam war as wrong and thus less authoritative. Similarly, the authority of the Supreme Court has vacillated markedly from time to time. Its resource of power has consistently been negligible, but when its authority is robust and inflated it would be difficult to exclude its leading justices from a list of the nation's political elites.

The distinction between authority and power is significant on two counts. On the one hand, it is likely that the primary source of elite status within industrial societies is authority, not power, and that the degree to which a particular elite is successful in expanding the scope of his authority is dependent upon the reaction of his constituents toward himself in general and the decisions which he makes in particular. Put somewhat differently, political elites are restrained by the bounds of their authority which in large part are determined by the reactions of the public toward them. This does not imply that the authority enjoyed by established elites is constantly in jeopardy, but it suggests that nonelites, especially in a democracy, have the capacity, when aroused, to curtail drastically, if not to bring down, elites whom they disfavor. The "crisis of authority" within major universities throughout the world, within the Catholic Church, and in American cities is a current instance of this phenomenon.

On the other hand, in the case of certain political elites, authority is not only the primary source of their elite status but also serves to free them from restraints otherwise normally imposed. In the United States, such elites primarily consist of heads of giant corporations. The magnitude of authority which the leaders of these institutions are able to exercise is well known.[7] Their decisions have a profound impact not only on the business cycle, on the allocation of human and economic resources throughout the country, and on the tastes and habits of the population, but also on the scope and nature of public policy. It is no exaggeration to say that the technostructure plays a major role in interacting with government in shaping and allocating social values.[8] Despite the objective evidence to the contrary, the American people deem corporate elites outside of the political realm and therefore immune from democratic standards and practices. Fortified by the myth of the free enterprise system, these richly endowed political elites are relatively free to render authoritative decisions on questions affecting the nation's well-being and are mostly accountable to themselves only.

In sum, the phenomenon of authority has had diverse effects on two classes of political elites: it has tended, although imperfectly, on the one hand, to restrain governmental elites within the bounds of what the public regards as legitimate and reasonable, and, on the other, to grant decision-making prerogatives of considerable magnitude to corporate elites with little regard to political accountability. But what is common to both is that the source of elite status is chiefly authority rather than power. This, of course, does not mean that power is an unimportant instrument in the creation, retention, or expansion of an elite position. Power is especially important when it is utilized by an elite, as it almost always is, in conjunction with authority. A president, a secretary of defense, a corporate executive, or any other head of a bureaucracy, would hardly refrain from exploiting the bureaucratic resources of power at his disposal as the person in authority. His strategy could well be to utilize each with the objective of expanding the other.

Second, aside from ignoring authority in the definition of the elite concept, Lasswell's conception of elites as power holders is also defective in that it is a static formulation. It is true that under normal conditions political elites have considerable power and authority to make decisions free from the pressures of their constituents. But during more turbulent times when nonelites become politically active, elite power as well as authority dramatically recedes. It is not uncommon, as Mosca and Pareto feared, that social movements of popular discontent breed new elites that challenge the rule of the old order. In these periods elite power is shared or simply transferred to a new set of elites. Nevertheless, social upheaval does occur, especially in its early stages, which is characterized by a substantial shift in power from established elites to nonelites. Defiance of the rules and procedures of the establishment and the threat to resort to violence, which are the two principal sources of nonelite power, have the capacity of drastically limiting the options of elites. The common response of either compliance to nonelite demands or defiance of these demands by a resort to violence is fraught with danger. Concessions may well be interpreted as a sign of weakness that triggers further defiance and bolder action by nonelites. To counter by the use of force may well enlarge and intensify the conflict. Either course, which recent events in France and the United States make clear, can jeopardize the privileged position of key elites.

The point that social movements are likely to lead to a serious decline in elite power and authority cannot be pushed too far. The rapid rise of power among nonelites during periods of social tension and turmoil is often a momentary phenomenon which is matched by an equally rapid decline in nonelite power. The strategy of confrontation—sit-ins, the seizure of buildings, and the like—that is commonly employed by nonelites is effective in creating a crisis situation that often results in significant gains for nonelites—at least they appear to be so at the time. But these gains are often illusory. An elite that is under attack remains unscathed in the long run if it is able to ride out the crisis and yield only on issues that do not seriously erode its permanent source of power and authority. On the other hand, if the elite is compelled to yield in this crucial area, the outcome of the struggle may well represent a lasting and basic gain for nonelites.

It was this kind of consideration which Robert Michels overlooked in his formulation of the iron law of oligarchy.[9] Of course, an elite will exist as long as the source of its dominance—the existence and legitimacy of a hierarchical structure of a bureaucracy which it controls—remains untouched. But when this hierarchical structure itself is under attack, then the inevitability of continuing elite rule by either an established or a new elite is open to question. At least this is the belief of current radical theorists, such as Arnold Kaufman,[10] who advocate the adoption of the principles of participatory democracy in a wide variety of bureaucratic institutions.

When viewed within a dynamic context, then, it is incorrect to perceive of political elites as comprising merely those persons who exercise a great amount of power (and authority) and the masses as exercising comparatively little. During periods of deep social discontent it would be more accurate to reverse the formula; elites, as formal decision-makers, exercise little power and authority, and nonelites exercise a great amount of power.

Finally, the traditional concept of elite is defective in that it ignores a significant attribute of elite power—the capacity of elites to make decisions through the form, paradoxically, of making nondecisions. An elite not only wields an inordinate amount of power in making decisions to initiate, approve, or veto policies within the scope of his influence, but he also exercises a great amount of power by *preventing* issues from being publicly considered that might threaten his interests. The exertion of power to achieve the latter objective may properly be called nondecision-making.[11] Clearly the more effective way to maintain the status quo is to prevent a radical proposal for change from developing into a public controversy than to attempt defeat of that proposal once it has aroused widespread interest. Adhering to this idea, a Supreme Court justice in a famous case after the First World War observed that it was safer and indeed more efficient to stamp out a revolutionary spark *before* it kindled a flame than to wait until it created a conflagration.[12]

Whether it is the proper role of political elites in a democracy to exert power to prevent issues considered potentially threatening to them from reaching the public arena is not my concern at the moment. Here my intent is to underscore the importance of this use of elite power. It is important not only because of its ability to narrow significantly the scope and nature of public controversy but also because power utilized in this form is usually exercised covertly, far removed from the glare of the public. Although the nondecision-making maneuvers that silenced the anti-Vietnam war position during the National Democratic Convention in 1968 were an exception in this respect, being done in the full light of the television audience, it is not improbable that this effort had a significant effect on both the breadth and intensity of the debate on the war during the ensuing campaign.

In sum, the customary power orientation to the concept of elite is in error both because it under- and overstates what is actually the case. It is understatement, first, because it ignores authority, which in most instances overshadows power as a source of elite influence, and, second, because it overlooks nondecision-making as a crucial means of sustaining elite power and authority. It is an overstatement because it does not take into account the capacity of nonelites to wield power in periods of social discontent. To assume that the masses *continually* are politically passive and relatively powerless is to ignore the dynamics of democratic politics.

I do not believe that any concise definition of the concept of political elite can be drawn that would adequately include all the essential factors, under changing social and political conditions. Following the practice often resorted to by economists, perhaps the best approach is to offer two static definitions that are applicable to two different social and political conditions. During periods of relative social and political tranquility, political elites comprise those persons who regularly exercise a significant amount of authority and power in making decisions and nondecisions that affect a significant number of people. During tumultuous social and political periods, a distinction must be made between established elites and new elites which tend to challenge the existing order. Established elites comprise those persons whose scope of influence and effectiveness remains relatively the same as in the past as well as those who experience a substantial curtailment in their capacity to exercise power and authority but who nevertheless continue to participate in making decisions. In a sense, the latter share the fate of kings who reign but do not rule. Their continuing elite status turns on their ability to maintain their positions and, once the crisis has subsided, to recoup and utilize their former sources of authority and power. Emerging or new elites, which challenge the established order, comprise those persons who exercise an inordinate amount of power which is directed against established elites and whose source of power in large part is derived from their ability to exercise widespread authority among nonelites.

II

I doubt if there exists a more striking illustration of Hegel's dialectic than the interaction between democratic and elite theories that has occurred over the course of the past two hundred years. Beginning with the attack against hereditary aristocracy by Machiavelli and Hobbes, neither of whom were democrats, theorists of democratic persuasion from Rousseau to Paine and Jefferson appeared to demolish the claim to rule by the rich, the wise, and the wellborn. But with the growth of industry and bureaucracy, both of which called upon the skills of the administrator and expert, and the apparent gap between the democratic ideal and the practice of elite rule, the elitist writings of Saint-Simon and Michels on the left, and Mosca and Pareto on the right, very much deflated the anti-elitist position of the democrats. The elite-democratic controversy appeared at a standoff for many years until quite recently when American social scientists, drawing upon both schools of thought, developed a theory of democratic elitism. This synthesis has been accepted by a broad range of scholars in both America and Europe. Its appeal is due largely, I suspect, to its realistic cast. It is a theory which is chiefly explanatory rather than normative, a theory which is based upon principles that are, in large part, adhered to in politics that are generally recognized as being democratic. In the process of forming this synthetic theory, the overriding question was no longer centered, as it had previously been among classical democratic theorists, on the ideals and aims that could serve as guide lines for an inspiring democracy, but rather upon the operating rules and principles that are an integral part of the political process of ongoing democracies.

The realists, such as Joseph Schumpeter, argued that democracy should not be conceived as a political theory that encompassed both ends and means, that democracy is solely "a political *method* . . . for arriving at political decisions in which individuals acquire the power to decide by means of a competitive struggle for the people's vote."[13] In driving home his point, Schumpeter asserted, "Democracy means only that the people have the opportunity of accepting or refusing the men who are to rule them."[14] With one stroke of the pen he fundamentally reversed the role of elites and nonelites as conceived by classical theorists. The latter regarded the democratic process principally as a means by which the moral and intellectual capacities of the common man could develop as he became involved and active in participating in decisions affecting himself and the community. The emphasis upon the self-development of the ordinary individual did not preclude guidance and encouragement by elites, but it did preclude a relationship of elite domination and creativity and nonelite submissiveness and passivity.

The difficulty with the classical theory, as underscored by the realists, was that it had little relationship to the real world. The evidence compiled by various studies consistently showed that the majority of people are politically apathetic and ignorant and that they simply do not choose to participate actively in political life. Confronted by this evidence, the contemporary democratic theorist had the option of embracing a normative theory of democracy which has little resemblance to the real world or of revising the theory to accord with the prevailing facts. In choosing the later course, leading theorists, in following Schumpeter, accepted and built upon what they took to be the dominant characteristic of the modern democratic polity—that minorities "counted for much and lead" and that majorities "do not count for much and follow."[15]

An impressive array of contemporary political theorists, including Harold Lasswell and Robert Dahl in the United States, Raymond Aron in France, John Plamenatz in England, and Giovanni Sartori in Italy, have been emphatic in insisting that the dominance of political elites in no way undermines or threatens the democratic process. The crucial point, which they are quick to underscore, is that multiple political elites in a democrary—as distinguished from a system ruled by a single and unified elite—compete vigorously among themselves on issues of public policy and for public office and thereby generate a basic restraint against the violation of democratic norms and rules by any one elite. Moreover, it is asserted, in their debate and struggle among themselves, elites fulfill an essential function within a democracy of presenting forcefully and articulately the alternative positions on pressing issues of the day. Without them, writes Professor Plamenatz, "there would be nothing worth calling public opinion; and in a democracy it is their business to make it without being able to decide what it shall be."[16]

As will be seen in several of the essays in this volume, this position is unconvincing to theorists who believe that a pluralistic elite system does not provide sufficient cohesiveness to guard against a takeover by a demagogue; to theorists who are not satisfied with a theory which explicitly emphasizes the importance of the stability of the political system and ignores its ability to provide the necessary political condition to advance the self-development of ordinary men and women; and to theorists who assert that the scope of elite debate within the existing system is limited to relatively unimportant issues that avoid the fundamental problems which confront contemporary society. The critics are in agreement that the realist's position is defective but are in wide disagreement as to what constitutes a viable theoretical alternative.

The pattern of ideological alignment centering on the elite-democratic issue cuts across both the traditional liberal-conservative and normative-empirical divisions. For example, among the authors included in this volume, both Herbert Marcuse and Paul Goodman regard themselves as radicals, yet on an elite-democratic spectrum their positions are far apart. Although Walker and Truman arrive at opposite conclusions, their attacks on the realist's position are along normative and empirical lines. To label either man on the basis of his essay as an empirical or normative theorist would be to place him in a procrustean bed. Berelson's and Dahl's essays, which, in my view, represent the realists' position, are clearly empirically oriented; nevertheless, the normatively based underpinnings of their argument can hardly be missed. The point is simply that an issue of this nature cannot be analyzed by relying on a preference for a radical or a conservative orientation, or a normative or an empirical approach. The reader will have to decide for himself what constitutes adequate criteria for reaching a sound position on this issue.

NOTES

1. "Power, Pluralism, and Democracy: A Modest Proposal" (a paper delivered at the 1964 annual meeting of the American Political Science Association, Chicago), p. 3.
2. For example, see T. B. Bottomore, *Elites and Society* (London, 1964), pp. 8–9; Giovanni Sartori, *Democratic Theory* (Detroit, 1962), p. 98; Marshall R. Singer, *The Emerging Elite: A Study of Political Leadership in Ceylon* (Cambridge, 1964), p. 5; and Suzanne Keller, "Elites," *International Encyclopedia of the Social Sciences*, vol. 5 (New York, 1968), p. 26.

3. *The Comparative Study of Elites,* with Daniel Lerner and C. Easton Rothwell (Stanford, 1952), p. 13.

4. With Abraham Kaplan, *Power and Society* (New Haven, 1950), p. 219.

5. See C. Wright Mills, *The Power Elite* (New York, 1956).

6. Lasswell defines authority as formal power rather than distinguishing it from power. See *Power and Society,* pp. 133–134.

7. See, for example, Arthur S. Miller, "Toward the 'Techno-Corporate' State?—An Essay in American Constitutionalism," *Villanova Law Review,* 14 (1968); and Grant McConnell, *Private Power and American Democracy* (New York, 1966).

8. John Galbraith, *The New Industrial State* (New York, 1967), chap. 34.

9. See his *Political Parties* (Glencoe, Ill., 1949), especially Part 6.

10. *The Radical Liberal* (New York, 1968). See also Paul Goodman, *People or Personnel* (New York, 1963), a chapter of which is included in this book (pp. 116–137).

11. Peter Bachrach and Morton Baratz, "Two Faces of Power," *American Political Science Review,* 56 (1962), 947–952; and by the same authors, "Decisions and Nondecisions: An Analytical Framework," *ibid.,* 57 (1963), 632–642.

12. Justice Edward Sanford, *Gitlow* v. *New York,* 268 US 652 (1925).

13. *Capitalism, Socialism, and Democracy* (London, 1961 ed.), pp. 242, 269.

14. *Ibid.,* p. 285.

15. Sartori, *Democratic Theory,* p. 98.

16. "Electoral Studies and Democratic Theory," *Political Studies,* no. 6 (1958), 5.

1 : *The Elite Concept*

HAROLD D. LASSWELL
DANIEL LERNER
C. EASTON ROTHWELL

THE ELITE CONCEPT IN HISTORY

The elite concept fills a blank in the language of science and policy. Words standing close to it already have rather definite meanings. A "leader," for instance, is ordinarily understood to be a prominent and active person. All leaders collectively are the "leadership." What is lacking is a term to cover both the leadership and the strata of society from which leaders usually come. Consider Winston Churchill. No one hesitates to call him a leader and to recognize that he has been part of the leadership of England for a long time, even though he was not always a leader. Nevertheless, even when too young to take part in public affairs, Churchill belonged to the political

From *The Comparative Study of Elites* (Cambridge, Mass.: Massachusetts Institute of Technology Press, 1965), pp. 3–19. Copyright © 1965 by The Massachusetts Institute of Technology Press. Reprinted by permission of the authors and publisher.

elite of his country, since he was born into one of the ruling families.

The concept of the elite is classificatory and descriptive, designating the holders of high positions in a given society. There are as many elites as there are values. Besides an *elite of power* (the political elite) there are *elites of wealth, respect,* and *knowledge* (to name but a few). Since we need a term for persons who are elite in relation to several values we speak of *"the* elite" (the elite of society). In democratic countries the political elite is recruited from a broad base. Elites in nondemocratic societies, on the contrary, spring from a narrow base, often from a few families.

It is true that the term elite has not been popular in democratic countries. In recent years Fascist, Nazi, and other nondemocratic movements have seized upon the word and given it a special twist for use as a weapon in the struggle for power. The elite, they say, is composed of persons with superior fitness to rule. They will and ought to rule. It is obvious, however, that no "ought" has scientific standing, since science is entirely concerned with "is." A scientist (and a democrat) can treat as a hypothesis the statement that individuals of great energy have an advantage in the struggle for power. Empirical connections between biology and power, however, cannot be transmogrified into a doctrine of "right to rule" which legitimately claims the sanction of science.

We need not take the fact too tragically that the term elite has often been misappropriated for doctrinal purposes, rather than left pure and free for the social sciences. A fact of life for social scientists is that many of the most convenient key words have "halo" effects arising from use in nonscientific circles. It is impracticable to expunge all halo words from the lexicon of the political and social sciences. It would be necessary to discard "democracy," "conservative," "liberal," "radical," "power," "political," "science," and a host of other terms. The only effective caution against halo effects is to develop scientists who are enough at home with the verbal tools of their craft to avoid being taken in by extraneous meanings.[1] Any new word introduced in place of elite would soon need laundering since whatever refers to a high position comes, by a process of generalization, to have normative connotations.[2] The "high" is equated with "very desirable."

The history of the term elite bears convincing witness to the generalizing mechanism just referred to. The word appears to have come into common use (at Geneva, Switzerland, for instance) as a means of designating choice merchandise, and was then extended to other objects "worthy of choice."[3] The idea of classifying people into groups, of which one is small and select, the other large and inferior, has many sources. One source is Jewish and Christian theology. It has long been common to speak of the "chosen people," the "elect" of God, and the "saints." Until quite recently it was taken for granted by the theologians of the Christian church, at least, that the majority of mankind would go to hell. Father Godts, for example, concluded after reviewing the testimony of Aquinas and others that "It is vain to seek even a single Saint who taught that the number of the elect form a majority."[4] The elite of God was indeed select.[5]

Before taking leave of the terminological aspect of the subject, it is worth noticing that some of the ill repute of the elite concept can be laid at the door of writers who, though attempting to employ the word objectively, have counterposed an incomplete conception of the elite to an even less adequate definition of democracy. The discovery that in all large-scale societies the decisions at any given time are typically in the hands of a small number of people affirms a basic fact. This is the sense in which, as James Bryce and many other political analysts have remarked, government is always government by the few, whether in the name of the few, the one, or the many. But this fact does not settle the question of the degree of democracy. To confuse the percentage of leaders at any given moment with the test of democracy is to make an elementary mistake, since *a society may be democratic and ex-*

press itself through a small leadership. The key question turns on accountability.

In partial extenuation of the writers who made one-sided applications of the elite concept during the century, it should be said that they were studying great states, where the elite was recruited on a narrow basis, or mass organizations, where the narrowness of the base was obscured by ideology. Mosca, to choose a distinguished example, was set off on his productive line of thought by Taine's *Ancient Regime*.[6] Robert Michels showed in masterly fashion how the control of mass parties, even parties engaged in propagating democracy, could gravitate into a few hands.[7] If we go back to the modern scholar who can perhaps be said to have originated the elite conception, we find that, as often happens in the history of thought, Saint Simon was better balanced than some of his followers.[8]

THE POLITICAL ELITE

The first step in clarifying the elite concept is to provide a working definition of power. In the older vocabulary of political science, power was often talked about in terms of will. In response to current pressure to substitute "behavioristic" for "subjective" terms, words like "decision-making" have come into vogue. The "decision process" appears to combine subjective and behavioristic connotations and to imply phases of initiation, consideration, enactment, and enforcement. *A decision can be defined as a severely sanctioned choice.*

A heavy deprivation is expected to be imposed, or is imposed, against a deviationist. The deprivation involves any or all values. For example, there can be severe reductions of power (loss of office, disenfranchisement, loss of citizenship); of wealth (fines, confiscation); or of life itself (capital punishment). When statutes, ordinances, and awards are flouted or disregarded, they are not true decisions; we speak of them at best as presumptive decisions. *Power we can now define as sharing in decisions. (Obviously the degree of sharing can range from near zero to near 100.[9])*

If we could define a decision as "what officials decide" the task of locating leaders would be simple. Unhappily those who are called officials do not always make the severely sanctioned choices, and the severely sanctioned choices are not necessarily made by persons called officials. Hence *we distinguish between "authority" and "control,"* since the king who reigns may not rule and the elected governor may be subservient to the un-elected boss. Authority always carries with it some modicum of control, however tenuous; control may have no shred of authority. When expectations concerning who "ought" coincide with who "does," authority and control can be reached at the same address.[10]

Another complication arises from the difference between "actual" and "potential" power. The problem is acute when a revolutionary movement is coming to full tide but has not risen high enough to sweep ancient landmarks downstream. The usual criteria reveal that the traditional holders of power are greatly restricted in scope. But it is not yet clear how to estimate *potential power,* since the success of the revolution remains in doubt. In quieter times the discrepancies between power currently exercised and power which is potential are less great.

The search for the political elite may well begin with what is conventionally known as the government. Conventionally speaking, government is the institution which is so named by the members of the community in question. *Functionally,* however, *only the institution which makes the severely sanctioned choices can qualify.* Since the true decision-makers are not necessarily known at the beginning of research the investigator can select government in the conventional sense as a convenient starting point.

The first research operation is to identify the individuals who have held a given position during a selected period. It is then possible to calculate the rate of personal circulation, which is the number of individuals occupying the post per unit of time.

The second problem is to determine the rate of social circulation, which refers to the social and personal characteristics of those passing through a specified position during a given interval. *We are interested in the continuity (or discontinuity) of the social circulation.* If everybody moves up a notch when his superior dies, the continuity of recruitment is complete. It is attained by providing for immediate succession. Continuity can also be realized by modes of recruitment which prescribe more remote succession, as when a process of election picks individuals outside the immediate and formal hierarchy. Discontinuity occurs when the method of replacing personnel is changed, or when it yields a personnel with novel traits.

In deciding whether new types of leaders are appearing we look into social class characteristics. An analysis of the House of Commons which included seven general elections, for example, showed that the percentage of members coming from titled families was high and stable (40 per cent).[11] Other ties with the social structure are examined, such as wealth, occupation, and enlightenment (to mention only a few possibilities). We also consider the types of personality from which generals, legislators, judges, and other political personnel are recruited.

Having found the social circulation we can determine the representativeness of community leadership. During the past sixty years, for instance, over half of the presidents' cabinets have been lawyers (55 per cent). However, less than 1 per cent of the gainfully employed in the general population are lawyers and judges.[12] It is typical for the parliaments of Western powers to underrepresent certain elements in the population, such as manual workers, clerks, farmers, women, and young people.

We also consider the flexibility with which a given leadership adapts to the changing composition of the community, or to varying levels of social crisis. From an analysis of social circulation through important governmental posts in New York, we know that during such crises as wars, officeholders are recruited to an increasing degree from among the wealthy. During intercrisis periods the wealthy return to private life, leaving the field clear to persons originating in lower income groups.[13]

Further insight into the elite comes with the calculation of *interlocking* among positions. During the Fascist period in Italy it made sense to pay particular attention to the interlocking of various organs of government with the Fascist party, since it was possible to explain which agencies were rising or falling in influence on this basis.[14] (When persons or positions are described as rising or falling in influence, it is a matter of specifying the amount of vertical mobility involved.[15])

Which time periods are the most suitable for elite studies? Even though no consensus exists, it is often assumed that "about a generation" is meant. But the boundaries of a generation are not fixed. We might arbitrarily choose a year to mark "coming of age." If we take the twentieth or twenty-first year, a century divides conveniently into five generations. This pace is perhaps too fast, since the oncoming wave of twenty-year-olds does not press upon or begin seriously to displace the elder generation until after more age and experience have been acquired. By the mid-thirties enough influence have been amassed to penetrate some important posts. Hence the convention of counting three generations per century has sometimes been adhered to. In crises, however, old ways of doing things rapidly grow obsolete, and leaders are superannuated at a faster rate than usual. During quiet times, on the contrary, a given personnel persists longer than usual.[16]

No one clock serves the multifarious purposes of research on elites. Some inquiries are better served by gathering data by regular intervals of time and studying "chronological generations." For other research tasks a "functional generation" is more illuminating, since it is described according to varying phases of social adjustment. A functional example is the "revolutionary generation" of 1917, meaning the leaders who appeared during the first seizure and defense of power and under whose direction the initial steps were taken toward industrializing Russia. The "Stalinist generation" is another functional case, referring to those in top positions after Stalin entrenched himself in command of the Party.[17]

Among the personal and social characteristics of an elite which are worthy of separate examination must be included *the means by which the active members of a ruling class reach the very top positions, or, contrariwise, fail.* Not all members of a ruling class, as implied before, take an active role or even an interest in politics. The point comes out plainly if we inspect a sample of 100 families of the British peerage in which the title has descended without interruption between 1800 and 1900. No less than thirty-one of these elite families were without known political activity. This was counterbalanced by the thirty-four families, two-thirds or more of whose members were active in politics. Since this sample was confined to the peers themselves, it is reasonable to assume that the degree of political interest has been understated rather than overstated.[18]

The systematic study of elites calls for information about *the values which are employed by the active members as the bases of authority and control.* (We speak of base values as the means; power, in this case, is the "scope" value sought.) Individuals born into the upper classes in any social structure that endures during their lifetimes are in possession of many assets of potential political importance. We know that an upper-class position often carries with it some formal share in politics. The upper position typically carries the advantage of *intimacy with the powerful* and a tradition (which is one form of enlightenment) about the strategy and tactics of rule. Besides, there is comparatively ready access to prestige, income, and other values.

We must specialize our examination of the active power elite by taking note of *the instrumentalities upon which they rely in advancing themselves* and *the usual ladder of rise* (*and decline*). What is involved are the skills (and the associated knowledge) utilized by the active and successful. Following current usage, it is convenient to classify the instruments of policy in a fourfold scheme according to the degree of reliance upon the manipulation of symbols or upon nonsymbols.

Diplomacy and propaganda depend upon words (and word equivalents). In diplomacy, the words are exchanged among elites (or elite members), while propaganda is addressed to large audiences of the rank and file. Economic and military policy usually involve the management of material resources and the coordination of human effort. We think of bargaining in the market and the management of production as representative economic skills, and military and police activity as specializations relating to violence. The negotiations of the diplomat and the bargaining of the businessman may both be "horse trading," as Bismarck put it, but they usually occur in a setting where the traders bear different relations to the horse.

Our conception of the "world revolution of our time" includes a number of hypotheses about the skills of elites and the design of the ladder climbed by the proficient. We shall emphasize the shifting correlation of influence among specialists on bargaining, violence, and symbols. Among the symbol specialists we pay particular heed to those who are devoted to propaganda or to such bureaucratic skills as the management of mass parties or the administration of official agencies. We look closely at the members of professions for which systematic training is requisite, such as law, and the more impressionistic intellectual activities which are closely connected with the humanistic tradition. We also consider the relationship between those engineering and technical skills which are connected with industrial methods of production, and the skills of the artisan and the peasant, which stem from a pre-industrial epoch. Among the symbol specialists we inquire into the relative influence of those who specialize upon sacred symbols and pastoral work and the ones who deal in secular symbols and social work. Our investigation must ultimately ramify through all branches of the healing arts and sciences, where the "medicine men," old and new, find their place in the sun or shade. Questions of this kind will be particularly rewarding when we examine the way in which folk cultures adjust themselves to the industrial pattern.

Because of the stress so often put upon the social origins

of an elite, and upon the path by which active members of an elite rise to the top, it is sometimes lost sight of that *origins are no infallible guide to eliteship. The essential condition to be fulfilled is accountability. To be accountable is to be influenced.* We are acquainted with the wide range of devices evolved by representative governments in their long struggle to control the executive and to keep all members of the active elite accountable to the passive elements of the ruling class. The devices include popular election of officials at frequent intervals; short official terms; initiative, referendum, recall; freedom of press; freedom to organize opposing (loyal) parties; freedom from coercion during campaigns and at the ballot box; separation of authority between branches of government; federation and devolution; substantive and procedural protections of the individual and of private associations from executive arbitrariness.

There is no body politic in which the active elite is wholly unaccountable to large circles within the community, and even to the community as a whole. Where means of peaceful influencing are not at hand, and deprivations are widespread, *attempts at enforcing accountability are likely to end in coercion,* whether in the form of assassination, uprising, sabotage, or civil disobedience.[19]

In what has gone before we have put the principal emphasis upon obtaining facts about the origins, skills, and accountability of elites. It is impossible to contemplate information of the kind we have been discussing without drawing inferences about the perspectives of elites. No one is at a loss to predict some of the dominant attitudes of an elite whose members have had experience in police work, and more especially in political police service, and whose numbers have been frequently decimated by peasant uprisings, assassination, and related means. Nor are we at a total loss for ideas about the outlook of an elite whose most active members come from old, landed aristocracy and who have rarely been the target of anything more serious than campaign epithets. However, we cannot verify these hypotheses short of conducting a direct examination of the utterances of elites. More than that, we cannot rationally infer from facts such as the nature of the skills employed by a revolutionary elite that the revolutionists necessarily possess a comprehensive theory of world history which is avowedly Marxian. We must turn to the direct scrutiny of elite utterances (and of the flow of communication through the body politic) to enlighten us on these and many other points.

In some ways the most important and tantalizing question about elites is the realism or fantasy of their perspectives. Individual members of a declining elite may recognize the nature of the changes that must be introduced if the elite is to sustain its position or to keep its losses at a minimum. These farseeing individuals are often unable to modify the prevailing outlook of their elite-mates, and disaster may ensue. Why is there both a realistic and a fantasy sub-elite?

Modern methods have provided us with research tools capable of being applied to the problem. One general hypothesis is that the realistic subdivisions of the elite have been recruited from those who have been in a position to acquaint themselves with emerging trends. This means that the focus of attention of the "realist" diverges from that of the "fantast." We may find that tutors or playmates, or travel abroad, give occasion for a new set of expectations, demands, or even identifications. However, this is not enough to explain all, since members of ruling groups can be exposed to similar opportunities without revising what they believe. Not only exposure but the pattern of predisposition at the time of exposure must be taken into account. We know that predispositions are screens to sift out the novel and disturbing, and to re-edit the current stream of incoming stimuli into old familiar grooves. The problem, thus narrowed, remains: what factors explain why some persons remain open to new and challenging experiences to which others (whose backgrounds are interchangeable in terms of class structure and culture) remain untouched? Much remains to be learned by intensive studies directed at the realistic and the fantasy sub-elites of a given ruling class.

The most intensive research on elites can focus directly on the question of distinctive elite practices. It is a question of the perspectives and operations revealed by the decision process. By proper methods it is possible to ascertain the "code" of an elite and to describe the values and objectives sought; the base values typically relied upon; and the detailed patterns of expectation, identification, and operation which are present. A scientific observer will take into consideration the principles and maxims made articulate among the decision-makers. In addition, the analyst will examine the mode of conduct displayed in typical circumstances, estimating the degree of elaboration and the intensity of all manifestations. Hence the "code" of an elite summarizes both conscious perspectives and unconscious demands, identifications, and expectations. The measure of intensity is the degree in which the total personality is involved. (By far the most thorough work of this kind is by Nathan Leites on the Politburo.[20])

In studying elites a word of caution may not be amiss. In the literature there are frequent references to the "pyramid" of power.[21] It should be clear that nothing inherent in the geometry of power restricts power to the pyramid. In innumerable situations, nevertheless, the pyramid is a faithful image of the prevailing pattern. When compared with the small elite cluster, other groups fall away toward the broad bottom layer of impotence or indifference. But power is not always concentrated in a few hands. When effective participation is widely dispersed it is more accurate to redraw the pyramid into a squat figure resembling a "flat-top" or a western "mesa." The group at the very bottom of the heap may be small, rather than large, so that the bottom of the pyramid must be pinched together and the whole figure redrawn nearer to the shape of a carrot. In any case the significant point is that elite patterns are to be discovered by research and not settled by arbitrary definition.

What has been said about the concept of political elite can be summed up as follows: *The political elite comprises the power holders of a body politic. The power holders include the leadership and the social formations from which leaders typically come, and to which accountability is maintained, during a given generation. In other words, the political elite is the top power class.* Obviously it does not include all members of the body politic unless everyone shares equally in the decision process. The extent of power sharing must be determined in every situation by research, since there is no universal pattern of power. *We speak of an open elite when all or a very considerable number of the members of a body politic are included. A closed elite, on the other hand, embraces only a few. A ruling caste is a ruling class closed to all save certain families.*

NOTES

1. Presumably one result of the new interest in logic, and in the expanding science of communication, will be to guarantee a high level of competence among scholars in the use of terms. From the voluminous literature the following represent significant currents: Charles W. Morris, *Signs, Language, and Behavior* (New York: Prentice-Hall, Inc., 1946); Kenneth Burke, *A Grammar of Motives* (New York: Prentice-Hall, Inc., 1945). Percy W. Bridgman, I. A. Richards, R. Carnap, Hans Reichenbach, and Alfred Korzybski are important contributors.

2. For the basic psychological mechanisms involved, see Clark L. Hull, *Principles of Behavior: An Introduction to Behavior Theory* (New York: D. Appleton-Century Company, Inc., 1943), chap. xii.

3. Renzo Sereno, "The Anti-Aristotelianism of Gaetano Mosca and its Fate," *Ethics*, XLVIII (1938), p. 515, footnote 15. Although Saint Simon made a clear statement and application of the concept of a ruling class, Mosca worked out the full significance of the category about 1883. There has been some animus over questions of priority as between Mosca and Pareto, with which Sereno deals.

4. Put in perspective by G. C. Coulton, *Mediaeval Panorama: The English Scene from Conquest to Reformation* (Cambridge: The University Press, 1944), pp. 417–418.

5. In Calvin's phrase, God's elect who are predestined to eternal salvation rather than eternal damnation owe all to "his gratuitous mercy, irrespective of human merit." *Institutes of the Christian Religion,* trans. J. Allen, 1838, Vol. II, pp. 128–29 (bk. iii, chap. xxi, paragraph 7).

6. Taine's book appeared in 1878; Mosca's first version of the elite was *Sulla teorica dei governi e governo parlamentare,* in 1884.

7. *Zur Soziologie des Parteiwesens in der modernen Demokratie* (Leipzig, 1911). The volume appeared in English in 1915 and has recently been reprinted by The Free Press, Glencoe, Illinois.

8. The contribution of Saint Simon is expressly underlined by Mosca, ". . . not only did he implicitly assert the inherent necessity of a ruling class. He explicitly proclaimed that that class has to possess the requisites and aptitudes most necessary to social leadership at a given time and in a given type of civilization." *The Ruling Class,* ed. A. Livingston (New York: McGraw-Hill Book Co., Inc., 1939), pp. 329–330.

9. For more detail consult H. D. Lasswell and Abraham Kaplan, *Power and Society: A Framework for Political Inquiry* (New Haven, Conn.: Yale University Press, 1950).

10. Sir Frederick Pollock distinguished between "legal" and "political" sovereignty in *An Introduction to the History of the Science of Politics* (London: Macmillan and Company, Ltd., 1902), p. 105. Parallel distinctions were made by James Bryce, A. V. Dicey, and many other writers.

11. J. F. Ross, *Parliamentary Representation* (London: Eyre and Spottiswoode, 1943), p. 80.

12. Consult Richard Fisher, *The American Executive: 1890–1950,* Hoover Institute Studies, Series B, No. 5.

13. Gabriel A. Almond, "Wealth and Politics in New York City" (unpublished Ph.D. dissertation, University of Chicago).

14. See "The Changing Italian Elite" (with Renzo Sereno), reprinted in H. D. Lasswell, *The Analysis of Political Behaviour: An Empirical Approach* (New York: Oxford University Press, 1949), chap. iii.

15. Consult P. A. Sorokin, *Social Mobility* (New York: Harper & Brothers, 1927) and the investigations thereby stimulated.

16. Arthur M. Schlesinger initiated useful research in American history by stressing the shift of generations. See his *New Viewpoints in American History* (New York: The Macmillan Company, 1922).

17. Consult George K. Schueller, *The Politburo,* Hoover Institute Studies, Series B, No. 2.

18. W. L. Guttsman, "The Changing Social Structure of the British Political Elite, 1886–1935," *British Journal of Sociology,* II (1951), 122–134.

19. On informal means of influencing an active elite see Charles E. Merriam, *Political Power: Its Composition and Incidence* (New York: Whittlesey House, 1934). This was reprinted in H. D. Lasswell, C. E. Merriam, and T. V. Smith, *A Study of Power* (Glencoe, Ill.: The Free Press, 1950).

20. A preliminary summary of Leites' results is in his *The Operational Code of the Politburo* (New York: McGraw-Hill Book Company, Inc., 1951).

21. For instance, chap. v of Robert M. MacIver's *The Web of Government* (New York: The Macmillan Company, 1948) is called "The Pyramid of Power."

2: *Democratic Practice and Democratic Theory*

BERNARD BERELSON

PAUL LAZARSFELD

WILLIAM McPHEE

What does all this mean for the political theory of democracy? For we have been studying not how people come to make choices in general but how they make a political choice, and the political content of the study has broad ramifications beyond the technical interests. In the end, of course, we must leave such theoretical questions to the political theorists and the political philosophers. But the fact that they would not be at home in our empirical material has encouraged us to speak at least briefly to their concerns. Both theory and facts are needed. As Schumpeter says in *Capitalism, Socialism and Democracy:* "The question whether [certain] conditions are fulfilled to the extent required in order to make democracy

From *Voting* (Chicago: University of Chicago Press, 1954), pp. 305–323. Copyright © 1954 by The University of Chicago Press. Reprinted by permission of the authors and the publisher. *Author's note:* The senior author is particularly indebted to his friend and colleague Edward Shils for stimulation and instruction on this topic in general and for advice on this chapter in particular.

27

work should not be answered by reckless assertion or equally reckless denial. It can be answered only by a laborious appraisal of a maze of conflicting evidence."

With respect to politics, empirical-analytic theory and normative theory have only recently become truly separated—and often to their mutual disadvantage and impoverishment. In a recent essay a British scholar comments on "The Decline of Political Theory." That there has been and is now a "decline" seems to be generally accepted. Why? Because, says Alfred Cobban, the theory of the great political thinkers of the past was written "with a practical purpose in mind. Their object was to influence actual political behavior. They wrote to condemn or support existing institutions, to justify a political system or persuade their fellow citizens to change it: because, in the last resort, they were concerned with the aims, the purposes of political society." He points out that John Stuart Mill tried to reconcile the demands for state action with established ideals of individual liberty, Bentham to establish a theoretical basis for the legislative and administrative reforms that were then urgently needed, Burke to provide an alternative to the new democratic principle of the sovereignty of the people, Locke to provide a political theory for a generation that had overthrown divine right and established parliamentary government, Hobbes to maintain the primacy of sovereignty in an age of civil wars, etc. From being "formerly the work of men intently concerned with practical issues," the study of political theory

> has become instead an academic discipline written in various esoteric jargons almost as though for the purpose of preventing it from being understood by those who, if they did understand it, might try to put it into practice. . . . Political theory has in this way become disengaged from political facts. Even worse, it has become disengaged on principle, as it has seldom if ever been in the past.

Here, it seems to us, lies one potential use of our data. If the political theorists do not engage directly in politics, they might explore the relevance, the implications, and the meaning of such empirical facts as are contained in this and similar studies. Political theory written with reference to practice has the advantage that its categories are the categories in which political life really occurs. And, in turn, relating research to problems of normative theory would make such research more realistic and more pertinent to the problems of policy. At the same time, empirical research can help to clarify the standards and correct the empirical presuppositions of normative theory. As a modest illustration, this concluding chapter of the volume turns to some of the broad normative and evaluative questions implied in this empirical study.

REQUIREMENTS FOR THE INDIVIDUAL

... the main impact of realistic research on contemporary politics has been to temper some of the requirements set by our traditional normative theory for the typical citizen. "Out of all this literature of political observation and analysis, which is relatively new," says Max Beloff, "there has come to exist a picture in our minds of the political scene which differs very considerably from that familiar to us from the classical texts of democratic politics."

Experienced observers have long known, of course, that the individual voter was not all that the theory of democracy requires of him. As Bryce put it:

> How little solidity and substance there is in the political or social beliefs of nineteen persons out of every twenty. These beliefs, when examined, mostly resolve themselves into two or three prejudices and aversions, two or three prepossessions for a particular party or section of a party, two or three phrases or catch-words suggesting or embodying arguments which the man who repeats them has not analyzed.

While our data do not support such an extreme statement, they do reveal that certain requirements commonly assumed for

the successful operation of democracy are not met by the behavior of the "average" citizen. The requirements, and our
conclusions concerning them, are quickly reviewed.[1]

Interest, discussion, motivation. The democratic citizen is
expected to be interested and to participate in political affairs.
His interest and participation can take such various forms as
reading and listening to campaign materials, working for the
candidate or the party, arguing politics, donating money, and
voting. In Elmira the majority of the people vote, but in
general they do not give evidence of sustained interest. Many
vote without real involvement in the election, and even the
party workers are not typically motivated by ideological concerns of plain civic duty.

If there is one characteristic for a democratic system (besides
the ballot itself) that is theoretically required, it is the capacity
for and the practice of discussion. "It is as true of the large
as of the small society," says Lindsay, "that its health depends
on the mutual understanding which discussion makes possible;
and that discussion is the only possible instrument of its democratic government." How much participation in political discussion there is in the community, what it is, and among
whom—these questions have been given answers in an earlier
chapter. In this instance there was little true discussion between the candidates, little in the newspaper commentary, little
between the voters and the official party representatives, some
within the electorate. On the grass-roots level there was more
talk than debate, and, at least inferentially, the talk had important effects upon voting, in reinforcing or activating the partisans if not in converting the opposition.

An assumption underlying the theory of democracy is that
the citizenry has a strong motivation for participation in political life. But it is a curious quality of voting behavior that
for large numbers of people motivation is weak if not almost
absent. It is assumed that this motivation would gain its
strength from the citizen's perception of the difference that
alternative decisions made to him. Now when a person buys
something or makes other decisions of daily life, there are

direct and immediate consequences for him. But for the bulk of the American people the voting decision is not followed by any direct, immediate, visible personal consequences. Most voters, organized or unorganized, are not in a position to foresee the distant and indirect consequences for themselves, let alone the society. The ballot is cast, and for most people that is the end of it. If their side is defeated, "it doesn't really matter."

Knowledge. The democratic citizen is expected to be well informed about political affairs. He is supposed to know what the issues are, what their history is, what the relevant facts are, what alternatives are proposed, what the party stands for, what the likely consequences are. By such standards the voter falls short. Even when he has the motivation, he finds it difficult to make decisions on the basis of full information when the subject is relatively simple and proximate; how can he do so when it is complex and remote? The citizen is not highly informed on details of the campaign, nor does he avoid a certain misperception of the political situation when it is to his psychological advantage to do so. The electorate's perception of what goes on in the campaign is colored by emotional feeling toward one or the other issue, candidate, party, or social group.

Principle. The democratic citizen is supposed to cast his vote on the basis of principle—not fortuitously or frivolously or implusively or habitually, but with reference to standards not only of his own interest but of the common good as well. Here, again, if this requirement is pushed at all strongly, it becomes an impossible demand on the democratic electorate.

Many voters vote not for principle in the usual sense but "for" a group to which they are attached—their group. The Catholic vote or the hereditary vote is explainable less as principle than as a traditional social allegiance. The ordinary voter, bewildered by the complexity of modern political problems, unable to determine clearly what the consequences are of alternative lines of action, remote from the arena, and incapable of bringing information to bear on principle, votes the way trusted people around him are voting. A British scholar,

Max Beloff, takes as the "chief lesson to be derived" from such studies:

> Election campaigns and the programs of the different parties have little to do with the ultimate result which is predetermined by influences acting upon groups of voters over a longer period. . . . This view has now become a working hypothesis with which all future thinking on this matter will have to concern itself. But if this is admitted, then obviously the picture of the voter as a person exercising conscious choice between alternative persons and alternative programs tends to disappear.

On the issues of the campaign there is a considerable amount of "don't know"—sometimes reflecting genuine indecision, more often meaning "don't care." Among those with opinions the partisans *agree* on most issues, criteria, expectations, and rules of the game. The supporters of the different sides disagree on only a few issues. Nor, for that matter, do the candidates themselves always join the issue sharply and clearly. The partisans do not agree overwhelmingly with their own party's position, or, rather, only the small minority of highly partisan do; the rest take a rather moderate position on the political considerations involved in an election.

Rationality. The democratic citizen is expected to exercise rational judgment in coming to his voting decision. He is expected to have arrived at his principles by reason and to have considered rationally the implications and alleged consequences of the alternative proposals of the contending parties. Political theorists and commentators have always exclaimed over the seeming contrast here between requirement and fulfillment. Even as sensible and hard-minded an observer as Schumpeter was extreme in his view:

> Even if there were no political groups trying to influence him, the typical citizen would in political matters tend to yield to extra-rational or irrational prejudice and impulse. The weakness of the rational processes he applies to politics and the absence of effective logical control over the results he arrives at would in themselves suffice to account for that. Moreover, simply because he is not "all there," he will relax his usual moral standards

as well and occasionally give in to dark urges which the conditions of private life help him to repress.

Here the problem is first to see just what is meant by rationality. The term, as a recent writer noted, "has enjoyed a long history which has bequeathed to it a legacy of ambiguity and confusion. . . . Any man may be excused when he is puzzled by the question how he ought to use the word and particularly how he ought to use it in relation to human conduct and politics." Several meanings can be differentiated.

It is not for us to certify a meaning. But even without a single meaning—with only the aura of the term—we can make some observations on the basis of our material. In any rigorous or narrow sense the voters are not highly rational; that is, most of them do not ratiocinate on the matter, e.g., to the extent that they do on the purchase of a car or a home. Nor do voters act rationally whose "principles" are held so tenaciously as to blind them to information and persuasion. Nor do they attach efficient means to explicit ends.

The fact that some people change their minds during a political campaign shows the existence of that open-mindedness usually considered a component of rationality. But among whom? Primarily among those who can "afford" a change of mind, in the sense that they have ties or attractions on both sides—the cross-pressured voters in the middle where rationality is supposed to take over from the extremes of partisan feeling. But it would hardly be proper to designate the unstable, uninterested, uncaring middle as the sole or the major possessor of rationality among the electorate. As Beloff points out: "It is likely that the marginal voter is someone who is so inadequately identified with one major set of interests or another and so remote, therefore, from the group-thinking out of which political attitudes arise, that his voting record is an illustration, not of superior wisdom, but of greater frivolity."

The upshot of this is that the usual analogy between the voting "decision" and the more or less carefully calculated decisions of consumers or businessmen or courts, incidentally, may be quite incorrect. For many voters political preferences may better be considered analogous to cultural tastes—in music, literature, recreational activities, dress, ethics, speech, social behavior. Consider the parallels between political preferences and general cultural tastes. Both have their origin in ethnic, sectional, class, and family traditions. Both exhibit stability and resistance to change for individuals but flexibility and adjustment over generations for the society as a whole. Both seem to be matters of sentiment and disposition rather than "reasoned preferences." While both are responsive to changed conditions and unusual stimuli, they are relatively invulnerable to direct argumentation and vulnerable to indirect social influences. Both are characterized more by faith than by conviction and by wishful expectation rather than by careful prediction of consequences. The preference for one party rather than another must be highly similar to the preference for one kind of literature or music rather than another, and the choice of the same political party every four years may be parallel to the choice of the same old standards of conduct in new social situations. In short, it appears that a sense of fitness is a more striking feature of political preference than reason and calculation.

If the democratic system depended solely on the qualifications of the individual voter, then it seems remarkable that democracies have survived through the centuries. After examining the detailed data on how individuals misperceive political reality or respond to irrelevant social influences, one wonders how a democracy ever solves its political problems. But when one considers the data in a broader perspective—how huge segments of the society adapt to political conditions affecting them or how the political system adjusts itself to changing conditions over long periods of time—he cannot fail to be impressed with the total result. Where the rational citizen seems to abdicate, nevertheless angels seem to tread.

The eminent judge Learned Hand, in a delightful essay on

"Democracy: Its Presumptions and Reality," comes to essentially this conclusion:

> I do not know how it is with you, but for myself I generally give up at the outset. The simplest problems which come up from day to day seem to me quite unanswerable as soon as I try to get below the surface. . . . My vote is one of the most unimportant acts of my life; if I were to acquaint myself with the matters on which it ought really to depend, if I were to try to get a judgment on which I was willing to risk affairs of even the smallest moment, I should be doing nothing else, and that seems a fatuous conclusion to a fatuous undertaking.

Yet he recognizes the paradox—somehow the system not only works on the most difficult and complex questions but often works with distinction. "For, abuse it as you will, it gives a bloodless measure of social forces—bloodless, have you thought of that?—a means of continuity, a principle of stability, a relief from the paralyzing terror of revolution."

Justice Hand concludes that we have "outgrown" the conditions assumed in traditional democratic theory and that "the theory has ceased to work." And yet, the system that has grown out of classic democratic theory, and, in this country, out of quite different and even elementary social conditions, does continue to work—perhaps even more vigorously and effectively than ever.

That is the paradox. *Individual voters* today seem unable to satisfy the requirements for a democratic system of government outlined by political theorists. But the *system of democracy* does meet certain requirements for a going political organization. The individual members may not meet all the standards, but the whole nevertheless survives and grows. This suggests that where the classic theory is defective is in its concentration on the *individual citizen*. What are undervalued are certain collective properties that reside in the electorate as a whole and in the political and social system in which it functions.

The political philosophy we have inherited, then, has given more consideration to the virtues of the typical citizen of the democracy than to the working of the *system* as a whole. Moreover, when it dealt with the system, it mainly considered the single constitutive institutions of the system, not those general features necessary if the institutions are to work as required. For example, the rule of law, representative government, periodic elections, the party system, and the several freedoms of discussion, press, association, and assembly have all been examined by political philosophers seeking to clarify and to justify the idea of political democracy. But liberal democracy is more than a political system in which individual voters and political institutions operate. For political democracy to survive, other features are required: the intensity of conflict must be limited, the rate of change must be restrained, stability in the social and economic structure must be maintained, a pluralistic social organization must exist, and a basic consensus must bind together the contending parties.

Such features of the system of political democracy belong neither to the constitutive institutions nor to the individual voter. It might be said they they form the atmosphere or the environment in which both operate. In any case, such features have not been carefully considered by political philosophers, and it is on these broader properties of the democratic political system that more reflection and study by political theory is called for. In the most tentative fashion let us explore the values of the political system, as they involve the electorate, in the light of the foregoing considerations.

REQUIREMENTS FOR THE SYSTEM

Underlying the paradox is an assumption that the population is homogeneous socially and should be homogeneous politically: that everybody is about the same in relevant social characteristics; that, if something is a political virtue (like interest in the election), then everyone should have it; that there is such a thing as "the" typical citizen on whom uniform requirements can be imposed. The tendency of classic democratic literature to work with an image of "the" voter was never justified. For, as we will attempt to illustrate here, some of the most important requirements that democratic values impose on a system require a voting population that is not homogeneous but heterogeneous in its political qualities.

The need for heterogeneity arises from the contradictory functions we expect our voting system to serve. We expect the political system to adjust itself and our affairs to changing conditions; yet we demand too that it display a high degree of stability. We expect the contending interests and parties to pursue their ends vigorously and the voters to care; yet, after the election is over, we expect reconciliation. We expect the voting outcome to serve what is best for the community; yet we do not want disinterested voting unattached to the purposes and interests of different segments of that community. We want voters to express their own free and self-determined choices; yet, for the good of the community, we would like voters to avail themselves of the best information and guidance available from the groups and leaders around them. We expect a high degree of rationality to prevail in the decision; but were all irrationality and mythology absent, and all ends pursued by the most coldly rational selection of political means, it is doubtful if the system would hold together.

In short, our electoral system calls for apparently incompatible properties—which, although they cannot all reside in each individual voter, can (and do) reside in a heterogeneous electorate. What seems to be required of the electorate as a whole is a *distribution* of qualities along important dimensions. We need some people who are active in a certain respect, others in the middle, and still others passive. The contradictory things we want from the total require that the parts be different. This can be illustrated by taking up a number of important dimensions by which an electorate might be characterized.

Involvement and Indifference

How could a mass democracy work if all the people were deeply involved in politics? Lack of interest by some people is not without its benefits, too. True, the highly interested voters vote more, and know more about the campaign, and read and listen more, and participate more; however, they are also less open to persuasion and less likely to change. Extreme interest goes with extreme partisanship and might culminate in rigid fanaticism that could destroy democratic processes if generalized throughout the community. Low affect toward the election—not caring much—underlies the resolution of many political problems; votes can be resolved into a two-party split instead of fragmented into many parties (the splinter parties of the left, for example, splinter because their advocates are *too* interested in politics). Low interest provides maneuvering room for political shifts necessary for a complex society in a period of rapid change. Compromise might be based upon sophisticated awareness of costs and returns—perhaps impossible to demand of a mass society—but it is more often induced by indifference. Some people are and should be highly interested in politics, but not everyone is or needs to be. Only the doctrinaire would deprecate the moderate indifference that facilitates compromise.

Hence, an important balance between action motivated by strong sentiments and action with little passion behind it is obtained by heterogeneity within the electorate. Balance of this sort is, in practice, met by a distribution of voters rather than by a homogeneous collection of "ideal" citizens.

Stability and Flexibility

A similar dimension along which an electorate might be characterized is stability-flexibility. The need for change and adaptation is clear, and the need for stability ought equally to be (especially from observation of current democratic practice in, say, certain Latin American countries).

How is political stability achieved? There are a number of social sources of political stability: the training of the younger generation before it is old enough to care much about the matter, the natural selection that surrounds the individual voter with families and friends who reinforce his own inclinations, the tendency to adjust in favor of the majority of the group, the self-perpetuating tendency of political traditions among ethnic and class and regional strata where like-minded people find themselves socially together. Political stability is based upon social stability. Family traditions, personal associations, status-related organizational memberships, ethnic affiliations, socioeconomic strata—such ties for the individual do not change rapidly or sharply, and since his vote is so importantly a product of them, neither does it. In effect, a large part of the study of voting deals not with why votes change but rather with why they do not.

In addition, the varying conditions facing the country, the varying political appeals made to the electorate, and the varying dispositions of the voters activated by these stimuli—these, combined with the long-lasting nature of the political loyalties they instil, produce an important cohesion within the system. For example, the tendencies operating in 1948 electoral decisions not only were built up in the New Deal and Fair Deal era but also dated back to parental and grandparental loyalties, to religious and ethnic cleavages of a past era, and to moribund sectional and community conflicts. Thus, in a very real sense any particular election is a composite of various elections and various political and social events. People vote for a President on a given November day, but their choice is made not simply on the basis of what has happened in the preceding months or even four years; in 1948 some people were in effect voting on the internationalism issue of 1940, others on the depression issues of 1932, and some, indeed, on the slavery issues of 1860.

The vote is thus a kind of "moving average" of reactions to the political past. Voters carry over to each new election remnants of issues raised in previous elections—and so there is always an overlapping of old and new decisions that give a cohesion in time to the political system. Hence the composite decision "smooths out" political change. The people vote *in* the same election, but not all of them vote *on* it.

What of flexibility? Curiously, the voters least admirable when measured against individual requirements contribute most when measured against the aggregate requirement for flexibility. For those who change political preferences most readily are those who are least interested, who are subject to conflicting social pressures, who have inconsistent beliefs and erratic voting histories. Without them—if the decision were left only to the deeply concerned, well-integrated, consistently principled ideal citizens—the political system might easily prove too rigid to adapt to changing domestic and international conditions.

In fact, it may be that the very people who are most sensitive to changing social conditions are those most susceptible to political change. For, in either case, the people exposed to membership in overlapping strata, those whose former life-patterns are being broken up, those who are moving about socially or physically, those who are forming new families and new friendships—it is they who are open to adjustments of attitudes and tastes. They may be the least partisan and the least interested voters, but they perform a valuable function for the entire system. Here again is an instance in which an individual "inadequacy" provides a positive service for the society: The campaign can be a reaffirming force for the settled majority and a creative force for the unsettled minority. There is stability on both sides and flexibility in the middle.

Progress and Conservation

Closely related to the question of stability is the question of past versus future orientation of the system. In America a progressive outlook is highly valued, but, at the same time, so is a conservative one. Here a balance between the two is easily found in the party system and in the distribution of voters themselves from extreme conservatives to extreme liberals. But a balance between the two is also achieved by a distribution of political dispositions through time. There are periods of great political agitation (i.e., campaigns) alternating with periods of political dormancy. Paradoxically, the former—the campaign period—is likely to be an instrument of conservatism, often even of historical regression.

Many contemporary campaigns (not, however, 1952) must be stabilizing forces that activated past tendencies in individuals and reasserted past patterns of group voting. In 1948, for example, the middle-class Protestants reaffirmed their traditional Republican position, the working-class Protestants reverted toward their position of the 1930s, and the working-class Catholics toward their position not only of the 1930s but of a generation or more earlier. In this sense the campaign was a retreat away from new issues back toward old positions.

Political campaigns tend to make people more consistent both socially and psychologically; they vote more with their social groups and agree more with their own prior ideas on the issues. But new ideas and new alignments are in their infancy manifested by inconsistency psychologically and heterogeneity socially; they are almost by definition deviant and minority points of view. To the extent that they are inhibited by pressure or simply by knowledge of what is the proper (i.e., majority) point of view in a particular group, then the campaign period is not a time to look for the growth of important new trends.

This "regressive tendency" may appear as a reaction to intense propaganda during decisive times. The term "regressive" need not imply a reversion to less-developed, less-adaptive behavior; in fact, one might argue that the revival of a Democratic vote among workers was functional for their interests. What it refers to is simply the reactivation of prior dispositions—dispositions in politics that date back years and decades, often to a prior political era.

Its counterpart, of course, is what we believe to be an important potential for progress during the periods of relaxed tension and low-pressure political and social stimuli that are especially characteristic of America between political campaigns. The very tendency for Americans to neglect their political system most of the time—to be "campaign citizens" in the sense that many are "Sunday churchgoers"—is not without its values. Change may come best from relaxation.

Again, then, a balance (between preservation of the past and receptivity to the future) seems to be required of a democratic electorate. The heterogeneous electorate in itself provides a balance between liberalism and conservatism, and so does the sequence of political events from periods of drifting change to abrupt rallies back to the loyalties of earlier years.

Consensus and Cleavage

We have talked much in the text, and perhaps implied more, about consensus and cleavage. Although there were certain clusters of political opinion in Elmira, at the same time there were a number of opinions that did not break along class or party lines. American opinion on public issues is much too complex to be designated by such simple, single-minded labels as *the* housewife opinion or *the* young people's opinion or even *the* workers' opinion. If one uses as a base the central Republican-Democratic cleavage, then one finds numerous "contradictions" within individuals, within strata and groups, and within party supporters themselves. There are many issues presented, cafeteria-style, for the voter to choose from, and there are overlaps in opinion in every direction.

Similarly there are required *social* consensus and cleavage—in effect, pluralism—in politics. Such pluralism makes for enough consensus to hold the system together and enough cleavage to make it move. Too much consensus would be deadening and restrictive of liberty; too much cleavage would be destructive of the society as a whole.

Consider the pictures of the hypothetical relationships between political preference (e.g., party support) and a social characteristic as presented in this chart:

Percentage for Party Y, by Characteristic X

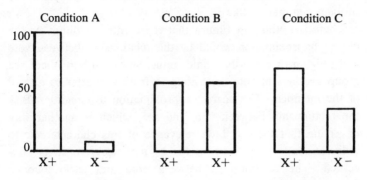

In Condition A there is virtual identity between the characteristic and political preference; all the people of type $X+$ vote one way, and all the people of $X-$ vote the other way. In Condition B the opposite is the case, and there is no relationship between vote and the characteristic; both parties are supported equally by people of the two types. In Condition C there is neither a complete relationship nor a complete absence; more $X+$'s than $X-$'s are partisans of a given side, but there are some members of each type in each political camp.

Now a democratic society in which Condition A was intensified would probably be in danger of its existence. The issues of politics would cut so deeply, be so keenly felt, and, especially, be so fully reinforced by other social identifications of the electorate as to threaten the basic consensus itself. This might be called "total politics"—a conception of politics, incidentally, advanced by such leading theorists of National Socialism and Communism as Carl Schmitt and Lenin. This involves the mutual reinforcement of political differences and other social distinctions meaningful to the citizen. The multiplication of Condition B, on the other hand, would suggest a community in which politics was of no "real" importance to the community, in which it was not associated with special interests. Condition C is a combination of Conditions A and B—that is, a situation in which special interests are of some but not of overriding importance. It portrays neither the extremist or fanatical community like A nor the "pure" or utopian community like B.

There is nothing in Elmira that represents Condition A; the closest approximation would be the relationship between vote and religion or minority ethnic status, and even here there are group overlaps in vote amounting to from a quarter to a third of the members. The nearest approximation to Condition B is the relationship between vote and sex, which is another way of saying that there is little relevance of this characteristic to political matters, at least so far as party preference is concerned. The relationships between vote and socioeconomic status or vote and occupation are examples of Condition C.

The social and political correlations we find in places like Elmira (that are not a priori meaningless) are of the C type to a greater or lesser extent. What this means is that there is a good deal of cross-group and cross-party identification and affiliation within the community. The political lines are drawn in meaningful ways but are not identical with the lines of social groupings. The same social heterogeneity that produces self-interest also produces a cross-cutting and harmonious community interest.

Thus again a requirement we might place on an electoral system—balance between total political war between segments of the society and total political indifference to group interests of that society—translates into varied requirements for different individuals. With respect to group or bloc voting, as with other aspects of political behavior, it is perhaps not unfortunate that "some do and some do not."

Individualism and Collectivism

Lord Bryce pointed out the difficulties in a theory of democracy that assumes that each citizen must himself be capable of voting intelligently:

Orthodox democratic theory assumes that every citizen has, or ought to have, thought out for himself certain opinions, i.e., ought to have a definite view, defensible by argument, of what the country needs, of what principles ought to be applied in governing it, of the man to whose hands the government ought to be entrusted. There are persons who talk, though certainly very few who act, as if they believed this theory, which may be compared to the theory of some ultra-Protestants that every good Christian has or ought to have . . . worked out for himself from the Bible a system of theology.

In the first place, however, the information available to the individual voter is not limited to that directly possessed by him. True, the individual casts his own personal ballot. But, as we have tried to indicate throughout this volume, that is perhaps the most individualized action he takes in an election. His vote is formed in the midst of his fellows in a sort of group decision—if, indeed, it may be called a decision at all—and the total information and knowledge possessed in the group's present and past generations can be made available for the group's choice. Here is where opinion-leading relationships, for example, play an active role.

Second, and probably more important, the individual voter may not have a great deal of detailed information, but he usually has picked up the crucial *general* information as part of his social learning itself. He may not know the parties' positions on the tariff, or who is for reciprocal trade treaties, or what are the differences on Asiatic policy, or how the parties split on civil rights, or how many security risks were exposed by whom. But he cannot live in an American community without knowing broadly where the parties stand. He has learned that the Republicans are more conservative and the Democrats more liberal—and he can locate his own sentiments and cast his vote accordingly. After all, he must vote for one or the other party, and, if he knows the big thing about the parties, he does not need to know all the little things. The basic role a party plays as an institution in American life is more important to his voting than a particular stand on a particular issue.

It would be unthinkable to try to maintain our present economic style of life without a complex system of delegating to others what we are not competent to do ourselves, without accepting and giving training to each other about what each is expected to do, without accepting our dependence on others in many spheres and taking responsibility for their dependence on us in some spheres. And, like it or not, to maintain our present political style of life, we may have to accept much the same interdependence with others in collective behavior. We have learned slowly in economic life that it is useful not to have everyone a butcher or a baker, any more than it is useful to have no one skilled in such activities. The same kind of division of labor—as repugnant as it may be in some respects to our individualistic tradition—is serving us well today in mass politics. There is an implicit division of political labor within the electorate.

CONCLUSION

In short, when we turn from requirements for "average" citizens to requirements for the survival of the total democratic system, we find it unnecessary for the individual voter to be an "average citizen" cast in the classic or any other single mold. With our increasingly complex and differentiated citzenry has grown up an equally complex political system, and it is perhaps not simply a fortunate accident that they have grown and prospered together.

But it is a dangerous act of mental complacency to assume that conditions found surviving together are, therefore, positively "functional" for each other. The apathetic segment of America probably has helped to hold the system together and cushioned the shock of disagreement, adjustment, and change. But that is not to say that we can stand apathy without limit. Similarly, there must be some limit to the degree of stability or nonadaptation that a political society can maintain and still survive in a changing world. And surely the quality and amount of conformity that is necessary and desirable can be exceeded, as it has been in times of war and in the present Communist scare, to the damage of the society itself and of the other societies with which it must survive in the world.

How can our analysis be reconciled with the classical theory of liberal political democracy? Is the theory "wrong"? Must it be discarded in favor of empirical political sociology? Must its ethical or normative content be dismissed as incompatible with the nature of modern man or of mass society? That is not our view. Rather, it seems to us that modern political theory of democracy stands in need of revision and not replacement by empirical sociology. The classical political philosophers were right in the direction of their assessment of the virtues of the citizen. But they demanded those virtues in too extreme or doctrinal a form. The voter does have some principles, he does have information and rationality, he does have interest—but he does not have them in the extreme, elaborate, comprehensive, or detailed form in which they were uniformly recommended by political philosophers. Like Justice Hand, the typical citizen has other interests in life, and it is good, even for the political system, that he pursues them. The classical requirements are more appropriate for the opinion leaders in the society, but even they do not meet them directly. Happily for the system, voters distribute themselves along a continuum:

Sociable Man   (indifferent to public affairs, nonpartisan, flexible . . .)   **Political Man**   *Ideological Man* (absorbed in public affairs, highly partisan, rigid . . .)

And it turns out that this distribution itself, with its internal checks and balances, can perform the functions and incorporate the same values ascribed by some theorists to each individual in the system as well as to the constitutive political institutions!

Twentieth-century political theory—both analytic and normative—will arise only from hard and long observation of the actual world of politics, closely identified with the deeper problems of practical politics. Values and the behavior they are meant to guide are not distinctly separate or separable parts of life as it is lived; and how Elmirans choose their governors is not completely unrelated to the considerations of how they are *supposed* to choose them. We disagree equally with those who believe that normative theory about the proper health of a democracy has nothing to gain from analytic studies like ours; with those who believe that the whole political tradition from Mill to Locke is irrelevant to our realistic understanding and assessment of modern democracy; or with those like Harold Laski who believe that "the decisions of men, when they come to choose their governors, are influenced by considerations which escape all scientific analysis."

We agree with Cobban: "For a century and a half the Western democracies have been living on the stock of basic political ideas that were last restated toward the end of the eighteenth century. That is a long time. . . . The gap thus formed between political facts and political ideas has steadily widened. It has taken a long time for the results to become evident; but now that we have seen what politics devoid of a contemporary moral and political theory means, it is possible that something may be done about it."

NOTE

1. A somewhat more general statement is contained in Bernard Berelson, "Democratic Theory and Public Opinion," *Public Opinion Quarterly,* XVI (Fall 1952), 313–330.

3 The American System in Crisis

DAVID B. TRUMAN

In the years since World War II the American political system has been subjected to a series of recurrent, almost chronic challenges whose implications may well cause thoughtful men to question the capacity of that system to survive. Two superficially dissimilar examples of these challenges are supplied by the crisis following the failure of our China policy in the late 1940's and the "Sputnik" crisis of October 1957.

The chief political significance of these events, perhaps, is that they were incomprehensible in terms of established American expectations—the China debacle because our experiences have given us little opportunity to reckon with honest, unintended, and perhaps even unavoidable failure, and Sputnik because we were utterly unprepared to confront the fact that

From *Political Science Quarterly*, 74 (1959), 481–497. Reprinted by permission of the author and publisher.

this could be a Soviet achievement, one not easily equaled by the United States.

Like any major event in human experience that is unexpected and, more important, lacks meaning—that is, cannot adequately be accommodated to established conceptions of reality —these produced a variety of responses, a good many of which were inappropriate in the sense that they were not adequately based on reality and hence could lead to entirely unintended consequences. Rapid, unpredicted change is always the enemy of stable and accurate perceptions, of established attitudes and loyalties. It leads to efforts, often at best frantic, to impose meaning on events and to grasp at compensating changes that are comforting because they seem plausible, that are psychologically useful though they may be realistically inappropriate.

Other events like Sputnik and the fall of China lie ahead of us for the indefinite future. The system that opposes us, while not our superior and probably not even our equal in basic capacity, appears capable for the time being, more than any despotism faced by us before, of an unrestrained concentration of energy and resources at particular points—such as rocketry and its associated technologies but not only in this realm—at which our vulnerabilities and the likelihood of embarrassment will be greatest.

The response of the United States to these events will be critically important in at least two respects. First, if our reactions are sufficiently inappropriate, they can lead to the disintegration and the destruction of the alliance that we lead. This is a prime target; the preferred objective of Soviet power is not the physical destruction of this country but the elimination of the leadership of the United States. The second respect in which our responses will be critically important is closely related but distinguishable, and it is the central concern of this essay. It is the danger of self-destruction, the danger that our reactions to frustrating and unexpected events will be so inappropriate to reality and their consequences so inadequately perceived that, in our efforts to increase our military strength and to fend off the intercontinental missiles, we may destroy the democratic system by which we live. Presumably one need not argue that this land as a prison of the human spirit would have lost its beauty as surely as if its cities had been laid waste and its population decimated.

This danger of self-destruction has often been pointed to, though perhaps of late a little less frequently than would be desirable. In any case, the present purpose is not to elaborate on it, but rather to look more narrowly at some misconceptions about the sources of the danger of self-destruction and about their character. The reason for this emphasis is that a number of eloquent and influential contemporary observers who seem to share this anxiety about the survival of our political system have adopted and publicized seriously mistaken views of where the danger lies and, consequently, of what is necessary to guard against it.

These views are best illustrated in Walter Lippmann's *Essays in the Public Philosophy,* which, upon its publication in 1955, caused considerable stir among readers of books and which one finds constantly cited as a source of confirming authority.[1] This book is not to be dismissed lightly. Lippmann's mind has always been an honestly troubled one, dealing with real questions; in this little book he is no less honest, and he is in such degree troubled that one may more accurately refer to him as tortured. Moreover, there is something in the substance of his argument, but that something has been so simplified analytically and so located philosophically that the result is at best unconvincing and at worst grossly misleading.

Lippmann's central thesis is a Spenglerian argument that the Western liberal democracies have been steadily declining both as powers in the world and as viable systems for conducting their own affairs. They are in serious danger both of being overwhelmed by totalitarian governments on the international scene and of being displaced within their own jurisdictions by counterrevolutionary dictatorships. The source of this "sickness" of the democracies he finds in the Jacobin surges of the nineteenth century that destroyed the authority of an educated governing class and, through the creation of large electorates, produced a domination of the government by mass opinion. This domination, first evident in the third year of World War I, reflects "a morbid derangement of the true functions of power."[2] "Prevailing mass opinion" prevents flexibility in making "hard decisions" by prohibiting changes in existing courses of action. "The people have imposed a veto upon the judgments of informed and responsible officials," and, "at the critical junctures," he argues, "prevailing public opinion has been destructively wrong."[3]

The chief institutional consequence of this mass domination has been "to devitalize, to enfeeble, and to eviscerate" the "congenitally" weaker executive power through the instrumentality of the representative assembly. Enormous expenditures, required primarily for war and reconstruction, have made the executive "elaborately dependent" on the assembly. At the same time "the growing incapacity of the large majority of the democratic peoples to believe in intangible realities" has "stripped the government [and chiefly the executive] of that imponderable authority which is derived from tradition, immemorial usage, consecration, veneration, prescription, prestige, heredity, hierarchy."[4] The result has been disaster in the affairs of the democratic nations and a "practical failure to govern" which, if continued, will lead to "counterrevolutionary measures for the establishment of strong government."[5]

The only remedy for these difficulties, Lippmann declares, is a return to the public philosophy, by which he means the natural law doctrine that reason can discover eternal and objectively true principles of justice by which the public interest can be validly determined in concrete situations. These, and not merely the positive laws of statute and constitution, are the laws to which all men, governors and governed, must be subject. Restoration of the public philosophy requires not simply an increased awareness of the social consequences of individual conduct and governmental policy. Rather it depends upon a "return" to the view that ideas and beliefs concerning "what man is and should be . . . , how he should hold himself in the scheme of things, what are his rightful ends and the

legitimate means" are matters of public concern. By a process
of subtle transformation we have moved, Mr. Lippmann thinks,
from the seventeenth- and eighteenth-century denial "both to
the state and to the established church [of] a sovereign
monopoly" in this realm to the view that these matters are
"private and subjective and publicly unaccountable." In consequence, "the liberal democracies of the West became the first
great society to treat as a private concern the formative beliefs that shape the character of its citizens." This has led to
the destruction of "a consensus on the first and last things."
The prudential policy of placing outside of the public domain
the "theological, moral, and ideological issues which divide
the Western society" could work only in a society such as the
Victorian, "which was secure, progressive, expanding, and un-
challenged." In face of the "hard decisions" of the twentieth
century, "the liberal democratic policy of public agnosticism
and practical neutrality in ultimate issues" is impossible.[6]

But the return to the public philosophy, to the view that
there is "a body of positive principles and precepts which a
good citizen cannot deny or ignore," is not directly a matter for
the mass of the population. "The public philosophy is addressed to the government of our appetites and passions by the
reasons of a second, civilized, and, therefore, acquired nature.
Therefore, the public philosophy cannot be popular."[7] It must
be adopted by the "men of light and leading," who are most
likely to be found in the executive and judicial branches of
government, if they are to have the moral courage to make the
hard decisions. It must also be taught to the masses if their
governors are to recapture the authority of imponderables, the
confidence and respect that will hold mass opinion in check.

It may seem inappropriate to challenge Lippmann's analysis and prescription exclusively on the American scene, since
his critique is applied to the Western democracies as a whole.
However, since he includes the United States and, indeed,
seems at times to single it out for special attention, it is not
unreasonable to argue that, if one can reject his observations
as they apply to this country, his entire position stands undem-

onstrated. It may well be, in fact, that a crucial flaw in his in-
dictment is precisely that he has drawn no distinctions among
the Western democracies but has treated them as essentially
identical systems suffering from a common disease.

One must grant, as I have already indicated, some validity
to Lippmann's concerns. The problem of securing far-sighted
leadership in a representative government is admittedly persistent; it may also be that this problem has been seriously
complicated by the movement in the past century from a
limited to a mass electorate, although one suspects that this is
an excessively simple explanation and that changes associated
with industrialization may be of greater relevance. One may
also concede that the survival of a constitutional system requires some degree of consensus on required and permissible
forms and purposes of political action and that the troubles of
some democracies can be traced to the weakness of such consensus. The fear expressed in this article, in fact, is that essential elements of the constitutional consensus in the United
States may be lost from view in the throes of convulsive response to external challenge.

But it does not follow that this consensus, to turn to that
matter first, must find its sanction in a doctrine of transcendental natural law which can or should be a positive guide to
determining the "public interest" in concrete situations. Natural law doctrines, even if widely shared by Mr. Lippmann's
giants of the seventeenth and eighteenth centuries, have never
provided precise determinations of particular issues. Surely it
is not for the want of adherence to a public philosophy, for
the absence of loyalty to the higher-law propositions of the
Constitution, or for the lack of judicial virtuosity that nine
honorable men on the Supreme Court have normally been unable to agree on preceisely what must be regarded as, in Mr.
Justice Cardozo's words, "the very essence of a scheme of
ordered liberty."

To insist that such doctrines can and must give positive
meanings over the full range of public policy necessarily leads,
as Lippmann rightly but rather blindly admits, to the impos-

sibility of a "policy of public agnosticism and practical neutrality in ultimate issues." But the abandonment of this policy of neutrality not only means that these matters are of public rather than private concern but also easily leads to authoritative determination of all such issues. By adopting his view we are likely to find the baby missing after the bath water has been disposed of. Lippmann does not go so far explicitly. He asserts, for example, that state and church must remain "separate, autonomous, and secure." But when he goes on to say that "on all the issues of good and evil" the two "must also meet" (the context not making it clear whether this verb means "to come into conflict" or "to agree"), he is dangerously close to asserting that these issues must be settled in terms of official doctrine, not on the basis of a careful assessment of empirical consequences.[8]

In his strictly political analysis, especially in his insistence upon the executive prerogative, he is also approaching advocacy of a kind of benevolent despotism in the guise of a set of Platonic guardians unhappily subject to the vagaries of popular election. He declares himself a "liberal democrat" who has no wish to disenfranchise his fellow citizens, and of the sincerity of this declaration one can have not the slightest doubt. Yet his Burkeian insistence on a "ruler" whose "duty is to the office and not to his electors," taken in the context of his portrait of the Western democracies as debauched and enfeebled by a willful, short-sighted, and dominant mass electorate, comes close to a rejection of his liberal democratic faith.[9]

Why should this be? Why should a man whose life richly deserves the respect of his fellow citizens, whose conduct amply testifies to his faith as a liberal democrat, be found confronting an unacknowledged dilemma between populism and authoritarianism? The question proposes no psychoanalytic examination of Mr. Lippmann, though one might be revealing, for the concern is with him as an example, not as an individual.

The answer or at least a large segment of it, lies in his conception—if one were to be malicious, one might say "stereotype"—of American society. In *The Public Philosophy* this conception contains only two terms: the governors, the "men of light and leading," and the mass, the people. Except for an occasional pejorative reference to "party bosses, the agents of pressure groups, and the magnates of the new media of mass communications," there is nowhere in the book a discussion of any intervening structure, of ranks of power and responsibility. Given his profound doubts—not in the slightest diminished since the publication of his *Public Opinion* more than thirty years ago—of the political capabilities of the ordinary citizen, his oversimplified social structure leaves him nowhere to turn, as the twentieth-century crisis deepens, except to his beleaguered executive as a source of authoritative myths and bold decisions. Curiously enough, he ends up in the same analytical position, though a very different prescriptive one, as some of the contemporary exponents of a conspiracy theory of American social structure, of whom C. Wright Mills is perhaps the most conspicuous example. Here too there are only a cohesive elite and a mass, with an inconsequential structure intervening. Power, to be sure, is ominously concentrated at opposing poles in the two conceptions of society, so that each observer fears the concentration that he sees, Lippmann the mass and Mills the "power elite."[10] Both cannot be correct. Neither can be more than partly so because each is working from a grossly oversimplified conception of the society.

The question is not whether one can share some of Mr. Lippmann's anxieties about the contemporary scene; the twin dangers, that inappropriate reactions to unexpected challenges might destroy our leadership in the free world and might equally destroy our democratic polity, are real. The crucial difference with him is rather with respect to the importance that should be attached to the intermediate social and political structure which he entirely omits from his analysis. This structure—which in simplest terms includes at least the great array of interest or pressure groups, corporations, trade unions, churches, and professional societies, the major media of communication, the political parties, and, in a sense, the principal state and local governments—this pluralistic structure is a central fact of the distribution of power in the society. It is a structure that is intervening between government at the national level and the rank and file of the population, intervening rather than subordinate or dominant. Within and among these groups, or rather their leading elements, a large fraction of the strengths and weaknesses of the American system is to be found. If one is disposed to engage in criticism and homilies, this structure must be a principal target. Much less is known about it than would be desirable, but enough is evident to indicate that it constitutes not only a distinctive feature of the American political scene but also a functional element of crucial importance in the system. In rough outline that system has for its frame the expedient of federalism, plus a few other formal arrangements, including the separation of powers and especially the less directly structural libertarian guarantees of the first eight amendments to the Constitution. New diversities of loyalty have developed to overlay, to reinforce, or to supplant those that faced the Philadelphia convention when the federalist compromise was drafted. Fragmentation, pluralism, and structural complexity have been encouraged by the basic framework and by a politics that was sheltered by the Hundred Years' Peace following 1815 and that for half a century after Reconstruction operated at the low temperatures friendly to the development of a complex industrial economy based on private initiative. The resulting political system is flexible, complicated, and peculiarly sensitive to the specialized demands emerging from its pluralistic base—specialized, however, in ways that may not be functional for the survival of the system.

The leading positions in the groups that make up the structure intervening between the government and the ordinary citizen obviously are centers of power, varying in importance, to be sure, but in the aggregate overwhelming. Less obvious but equally important, they are, in this kind of society, positions of responsibility and of privilege. One need not entirely share Lippmann's disbelief in the political capacities of the rank-and-file citizen to accept the axiom that a mass of people cannot act except through organization and in response to the initiatives of small numbers of leaders. Those who occupy leading positions within the groups constituting the intervening structure of American society are, in the technical and neutral sense of the term, elites. Being more influential, they are privileged; and, being privileged, they have, with few exceptions, a special stake in the continuation of the political system on which their privileges rest.

That stake, however, and those privileges may be apparent only to the analyst. For some elites this lack of awareness may derive from the relatively narrow range within which they are influential; for others, their positions not being overtly political, there may be no evident connection with the system of governing; and for still others, lack of awareness of their stake may be more a consequence of the fact that, though, as elites, they wield significant powers, the interests for which they speak are not yet granted full legitimacy in the larger society. Taken as a whole, these privileged leaders are not drawn from a single segment of the class structure, and, like other elite elements in American society, as Edward Shils has pointed out in his essay on *The Torments of Secrecy,* the geographic mobility that has attended their movement into positions of influence characteristically has denied them the security and the awareness that may be provided by traditional ties.[11] For these and other reasons, collectively they have few of the qualities of a self-conscious governing class. Moreover, many leaders in the intervening structure, perhaps especially those whose advancement has been rapid, have gained and held their positions only through an intense specialization, a single-minded concentration on the requirements of power within the group, that hardly encourages awareness of the larger system on which their power and privileges ultimately depend.

The hazards are great for any system that is chronically exposed to challenge and rapid change. But a system so exposed in which also a large proportion of the holders of power and privilege are unaware of their positions has special vulnerabilities. Foremost among these is the possibility that the members of these elites will not see a threat to the system for what it is. In such a scheme the substantive content of action —policies advocated and defended—is relatively close to the surface and easily perceived, especially by those elite elements whose specializations are closely related to the policies in question. Concern with that content, with the introduction and alteration of policy, necessarily involves conflict and struggle for substantial stakes. This conflict is inherent in the process, and it follows from the diversities within the society. Risk does not lie in the conflict as such, however, but in the possibility that the means by which it is carried on may violate the requirements of the system. For at bottom the system is a matter of procedure, not merely the formal procedures of adjudication or of legislative deliberation, but equally those involved in the free expression of demands and criticisms, in the legitimacy of dissent, and in unrestricted assembly and organization within the society at large. If, in the heat of controversy, some contestants, concerned more with substance than with process, deny the validity of these procedures for their opponents, and if other elements in this elite structure, preoccupied with the substance of their own specializations, acquiesce in this denial, the system as a whole is weakened. For, if the procedures may be arbitrarily denied to some, they cannot be assumed with assurance by any. Confidence in their availability is essential to the system; arbitrary and unpredictable denial has as its consequence a creeping loss of this confidence, encouraging a further resort to unstandardized and illegitimate means.

To expect a mutual esteem among all the elements of a loose and heterogeneous elite structure is probably unreasonable in a society where those elements are not based on the traditions of a common class. If those traditions are absent, a mutual attachment to the requirements of the system and a common concern for their protection become imperative. This attachment and this concern, however, need not rest upon the acceptance of Mr. Lippmann's public philosophy or its equivalent. They do not need to be derived from a set of eternal principles of justice. The word "need" is emphasized because it is not the intention to imply that anyone who *for himself* finds the authority for the system and his attachment to it in what he regards as eternal principles cannot as well as another identify a threat to it. But he cannot claim that his principles must be acknowledged before others can perform in the same way. Obviously the system rests at bottom on a respect for the dignity of man. This much is imperative; this much is indispensable. But beyond that no more is required than a pragmatic, humanist assessment of consequences. Rather than upon authoritative rules deduced from a transcendental doctrine, attachment to the system's requirements and concern for their protection can more easily and more hopefully rest upon understanding the nature of the system as it is, upon perception of the consequences for the system that are likely to follow from the actions of elite elements within it, and upon a willingness to act upon those perceptions in its defense.

A second vulnerability of an unself-conscious and loosely integrated elite structure is that, even if threats to the system are perceived, they may not be appropriately acted upon. The heart of this danger, as Gabriel Almond has pointed out in his discussion of elite behavior in the realm of foreign policy, is that looseness of the elite structure leaves unclear and unspecified, by formal prescription or established tradition, where the initiative in these matters must be taken.[12] This is evident enough in many areas of substantive policy. It is even more pertinent in those situations where the need is less for substantive policy than for resistance to encroachments upon the procedures on which the process rests. The two are interconnected, however, for the lack of a strong governmental initiative in the wake of unanticipated events, such as those referred to at the outset of these remarks, may invite its seizure by demagogic leaders whose actions may constitute a threat to the system of procedures. This is the point at which Mr. Lippmann's unstable public opinion becomes a problem, but not as a ruthless force dominating helpless legislatures and trampling on wise executives. A mood of anxiety, focused by unexpected change but unguided by customary instruments of leadership, is an invitation to initiative from novel sources not contained within the system and not restrained by its unwritten rules. An initiative thus boldly taken in matters of substance, moreover, especially when it is widely applauded, is more difficult to restrain if it reaches the point of challenging the system at its procedural heart. An initiative that has been lost in connection with substantive matters that are merely awkward and perplexing is not likely to be easily recaptured when to awkwardness must be added considerable unpopularity.

In this connection it is important to bear in mind that, though we are accustomed, and properly, to rely upon the executive and legislative branches of the national government to take the initiative both in the most important issues of substantive policy and in defense of the system's underlying procedures, this does not entirely take care of the matter. The total scheme, of which these governmental institutions are merely a part, is, as noted earlier, flexible, complicated, and highly reflective of specialized demands. Threatened conflicts between those demands, especially in the absence of a general elite consensus, can, even with an aggressive government, invite dangerous temporizing. It was not astonishing, for example, that Franklin Roosevelt, after the hostile reception given his "Quarantine" speech in 1937 by the press and other elite elements, was a good deal less eager to assume bold initiative in foreign policy matters. It may be less obvious that when an Administration-sponsored Senate investigation in 1950 into Senator McCarthy's charges against the State Department was followed by mercilessly unjust accusations against its chairman, Senator Tydings, and by his defeat in the election of that year, without significant repudiation of these tactics by the leaders of organized labor, especially in Maryland, of business groups, and of most of the press, there was little disposition in the executive or elsewhere in the government in this or the subsequent Administration to offer concerted and open challenge to the reckless demands of Senator McCarthy and his associates. Yet the explanations for these two political developments are strikingly parallel, and they do not lie within the government itself.

Ill-considered responses from within the intervening structure to an exploratory initiative from a major governmental source may lead to its relinquishing the initiative and to disastrous inaction capitalized upon by destructive leadership from another source. One of the hazards, and also potentially one of the strengths of the system as a whole, is that initiative can come from almost anywhere within it; one need not go through a long and elaborate period of training and seasoning in order to get a public hearing; co-optation, though increasingly common perhaps, is still not the characteristic method of recruitment throughout the system. But the possibility for rapid ascent and the diversity of paths to power within the system mean that any of several positions may provide the basis for an irresponsible initiative that under certain conditions may be parleyed into a force of monstrous destructiveness.

The essential point is that the system, including its governmental parts, must be recognized as a totality of interdependent elements. Neither responsibility nor privilege is distributed evenly over it, of course. At the governmental center both may be considerable. For the isolated voter at the periphery who has no special standing in groups of consequence, both responsibility and privilege perhaps are minimal. But over the reaches of the intervening structure, the intermediate leadership not considered in Lippmann's conception, privilege and responsibility are in the aggregate very great. In times of crisis the fate of the system may turn on whether both privilege and responsibility are satisfactorily acknowledged, not alone, or even primarily, in the governmental segment, but also and especially at all those points in the intervening "private" sector where the price of position and privilege is acceptance of the responsibility for a sharp perception of consequences. One can here appropriately apply to the government as a whole what Learned Hand some years ago said of an independent judiciary:

"a society so riven that the spirit of moderation is gone, no court can save; . . . a society where that spirit flourishes no court need save; . . . in a society which evades its responsibility by thrusting upon the courts the nurture of that spirit, that spirit in the end will perish."[13]

In events since World War II there is ample precedent for an anxious concern over the vitality of the elite structure in this country, specifically in that eruption recently so conspicuously associated with the name of the late Senator McCarthy. The word "associated" is used advisedly, for at its full flood this reactive movement was the creation, not so much of a single man, but of a society. Its parallels to what may lie ahead are frighteningly close. The movement was rooted in tensions that are deeply planted and its precipitating circumstances closely resembled the challenges to come: events at home and abroad that could not easily and comfortably be explained by established conceptions of reality, conceptions rooted in the worthy but dangerous assumption, not too much at variance with the history of this people, that all problems are soluble and that the solutions at which Americans arrive are inevitably superior. For the frustrations and miscarriages of of American policy in the world this movement in effect offered the reassuring explanation that such failures were not the consequence of honest mistakes and circumstances beyond the control of the United States but were the result of treachery, especially from within the government. This view acquired a certain plausibility from events such as the Hiss affair, and it seemed to be confirmed by the disclosure, a few months after the McCarthy meteor first appeared over the horizon, that the Soviet Union had achieved an atomic explosion.

The McCarthy career itself illustrates the striking possibilities of the system for rapid shifts in the sources of initiative. In less than five years this man moved from the comparative obscurity of his native state, untrained in national affairs and untested by their complicated demands, to a position as one of the most important figures on the Washington scene. This sort of ascent was not unprecedented, and almost certainly it will happen again. It is to be expected unless we introduce alterations in the political scheme more sweeping than any that one can reasonably expect or that one should desire. For, if there are risks in an unstandardized, diversified system of recruitment to positions of influence such as ours, a system whose normal paths may be spectacularly shortened by the bold newcomer, there are also risks in a scheme of co-optation and long apprenticeship, the risks of a timid gerontocracy.

The immediate challenge of the McCarthy movement was not its explanations nor its inexperienced leadership, but its radical constitutional doctrines, colorfully summarized in the Senator's observation, dismissing criticisms of his methods, that "You don't wear a silk hat on a skunk hunt." The materials of the "silk hat," of course, were such things as the proposition that a man, responsible for his own actions, shall not be condemned until he has been found guilty by the orderly processes of the law and shall not be punished by the arbitrary action of any official, no matter how worthy his motives; and the "skunks" that were pursued in this sporting event were, for the most part, American citizens entitled by law to the presumption of innocence and to due process, rightful inheritors of the tradition, without which free government cannot exist, that opposition and dissent are not automatically to be regarded as equivalent to disloyalty.

This was the challenge. The danger, however, lay less in the challenge than in the response, throughout the system but especially in that segment loosely referred to here as the intervening structure of elites. The response in that segment during the years 1950 through 1954 was not reassuring. Though the evidence is not beyond contradiction, it seems clear that among the elites the threat was not generally seen for what it was. Samuel A. Stouffer's researches indicate that, on the level of attitudes, "community leaders are more likely than the rank and file to give the sober second thought to the civil rights of the nonconformists," but it is still reasonable to conclude that "I do not approve of his methods, but . . . " was not only a familiar comment but in most cases also an operational code of elite behavior.[14]

There was, of course, active support of "McCarthyism" in some quarters, such as the leaders of some veterans' organizations, of some para-religious groups, and even of some patriotic organizations whose purposes ostensibly dedicated them to constitutionalism. There was also support from individuals who were enjoying the material benefits of privilege without accepting its responsibilities. But more striking than these aspects of the response was, to put the matter in its best light, the slowness with which the elements of an unself-conscious elite mobilized in defense, even when the threat was accurately perceived. Four years may not ordinarily be a long time in the life of a people, but in a time of real crisis it may be just too long. In this instance it was very long. In fact, one may well question whether a significant mobilization of the elites ever took place. It is well to remember, as the Dean of one of our great law schools suggested in a recent address in which he called his profession to account for its inadequate public leadership, that these were days in which the organized bar of the United States "instead of setting an example of dedication to due process and providing guidance to the public as to the meaning of the Fifth Amendment was attempting to apply a severe sanction [disbarment] against the assertion by a member of the profession of his constitutional rights."[15]

Small wonder that when Senator McCarthy was brought to book by his colleagues it was on the narrow ground of offense against the code regulating one Senator's conduct toward another rather than on the broader basis of disregarding constitutional limitations. Small wonder also that passage of the censure resolution was delayed until after the midterm elections and that nearly a quarter of the Senators finally voting on the resolution opposed the action. Some Senators undoubtedly would not have given their assent under any conditions, but, in the absence of consensus among the nongovernmental elites on the nature of the challenge and the need for restraining action, it is astonishing that the Senate acted as vigorously as it did.

This kind of threat will come again, but it can never be more obvious than it was between 1950 and 1954. Precipitating events beyond our shores will perhaps be clearer and more insistent, but they will be no more easily understood than those that occurred in the five years after World War II. As they become more apparent, in fact, the danger increases that the response to frustration and anxiety will invite more strongly the threat of self-destruction.

Resistance to this threat cannot be expected from the mass of ordinary citizens, not because their "appetites and passions" are ungoverned by reason, and not because they are unattached to constitutional ideals when they know them to be threatened, but because the division of labor that exists in our political system does not locate among them the responsibility or even the opportunity directly to perceive the less obvious threats hidden in responses to events taking place in an unfriendly spot halfway around the world. The theory of the omnicompetent citizen, with which Lippmann frightened himself nearly forty years ago, is his theory. It is not essential to the system. Robert MacIver has paraphrased one version of this notion: "How could . . . the democratic man have an effective opinion about the situation in China today and about the sewers in Brooklyn tomorrow, and the next day about some deal with Yugoslavia, and so on without end? He gave it up. He was disillusioned about democracy. He could not live up to its demands." MacIver's reply cut the ground from under this complaint without insult to the ordinary citizen: "If any 'man in the street' holds these views about his democratic obligations it is quite proper that he be disillusionized. But not . . . about democracy. Only about his illusions about democracy. Representative democracy . . . does not put any such impossible strain on the citizen."[16]

Nor can we, even if we would, wait upon Mr. Lippmann's executive elite, guided by his public philosophy. Appearance of the executive authority he looks for would require changes in the whole political system of which no signs are evident. Indeed, if this is the only way to survival, as he seems to think, we are assuredly doomed. The public philosophy as he describes it would fit only a golden-age view of the seventeenth and eighteenth centuries; it is even more out of place in a secular and scientific age.

The system, if we omit the unpredictable consequences of violent upheaval, must be taken as it is and understood as it is, subject to gradual modification but not susceptible to rapid and major alteration; and it must be taken whole, not merely in its governmental features but in its reach throughout the entire society. Within that system, owing to peculiarities of the governmental scheme proper, the challenge to political maturity and sophistication is peculiarly the lot of those in positions of privilege in the structure of elites intervening between the government as such and the ordinary citizen. The capacity of that structure to respond appropriately is the crucial matter. We can demand and with considerable assurance expect vision and initiative from within the governmental sector. But we cannot confidently expect to see these qualities of action governmentally unless they are supported from the ranks of the nongovernmental elites by a broad, consensual perception of the threats to the system that lie partially obscured in the responses to external events. Without that support the nation may survive, but the values embodied in its political system will be in constant jeopardy.

NOTES

1. Walter Lippmann, *Essays in the Public Philosophy* (Boston, 1955). References are to the Mentor edition (New York, 1956).
2. *Ibid.*, p. 19.
3. *Ibid.*, pp. 23–24.
4. *Ibid.*, pp. 43 and 49.
5. *Ibid.*, p. 53.
6. *Ibid.*, pp. 78–79.
7. *Ibid.*, p. 124.
8. *Ibid.*, p. 119.
9. *Ibid.*, pp. 18 and 46.

10. Cf. C. Wright Mills, *The Power Elite* (New York, 1956).
11. Edward A. Shils, *The Torments of Secrecy: The Background and Consequences of American Security Policies* (Glencoe, Ill., 1956), p. 79.
12. Gabriel A. Almond, *The American People and Foreign Policy* (New York, 1950), pp. 144 *et seq.*
13. *The Spirit of Liberty: Papers and Addresses of Learned Hand* (New York, 1952), p. 181.
14. Samuel A. Stouffer, *Communism, Conformity, and Civil Liberties* (New York, 1955), p. 57.
15. Jefferson B. Fordham, *The Legal Profession and American Constitutionalism* (New York, 1957), p. 23.
16. Robert M. MacIver, *The Ramparts We Guard* (New York, 1950), p. 27.

4: A Critique of the Elitist Theory of Democracy

JACK L. WALKER

During the last thirty years, there have been numerous attempts to revise or reconstitute the "classical" theory of democracy: the familiar doctrine of popular rule, patterned after the New England town meeting, which asserts that public policy should result from extensive, informed discussion and debate.[1] By extending general participation in decision-making the classical theorists hoped to increase the citizen's awareness of his moral and social responsibilities, reduce the danger of tyranny, and improve the quality of government. Public officials, acting as agents of the public at large, would then carrry out the broad policies decided upon by majority vote in popular assemblies.

Although it is seldom made clear just which of the classical democratic theorists is being referred to, contemporary criticism has focused primarily on the descriptive elements of

From *The American Political Science Review,* 60 (1966), 285–295. Reprinted by permission of the author and publisher.

the theory, on its basic conceptions of citizenship, representation, and decision-making.[2] The concept of an active, informed, democratic citizenry, the most distinctive feature of the traditional theory, is the principal object of attack. On empirical grounds it is argued that very few such people can be found in Western societies. Public policy is not the expression of the common good as conceived of by the citizenry after widespread discussion and compromise. This description of policy making is held to be dangerously naive because it overlooks the role of demagogic leadership, mass psychology, group coercion, and the influence of those who control concentrated economic power. In short, classical democratic theory is held to be unrealistic; first because it employs conceptions of the nature of man and the operation of society which are utopian, and second because it does not provide adequate, operational definitions of its key concepts.

Since contemporary scholars have found the classical theory of democracy inadequate, a "revisionist" movement has developed, much as it has among contemporary Marxists, seeking to reconstitute the theory and bring it into closer correspondence with the latest findings of empirical research. One major restatement, called the "elitist theory of democracy" by Seymour Martin Lipset,[3] is now employed in many contemporary books and articles on American politics and political behavior and is fast becoming part of the conventional wisdom of political science.

The adequacy of the elitist theory of democracy, both as a set of political norms and as a guide to empirical research, is open to serious question. It has two major shortcomings: first, in their quest for realism, the revisionists have fundamentally changed the normative significance of democracy, rendering it a more conservative doctrine in the process; second, the general acceptance of the elitist theory by contemporary political scientists has led them to neglect almost completely some profoundly important developments in American society.

NORMATIVE IMPLICATIONS OF THE ELITIST THEORY

At the heart of the elitist theory is a clear presumption of the average citizen's inadequacies. As a consequence, democratic systems must rely on the wisdom, loyalty, and skill of their political leaders, not on the population at large. The political system is divided into two groups: the *elite,* or the "political entrepreneurs,"[4] who possess ideological commitments and manipulative skills; and the *citizens at large,* the masses, or the "apolitical clay"[5] of the system, a much larger class of passive, inert followers who have little knowledge of public affairs and even less interest. The factor that distinguished democratic and authoritarian systems, according to this view, is the provision for limited, peaceful competition among members of the elite for the formal positions of leadership within the system. As Joseph Schumpeter summarized the theory: "the democratic method is that institutional arrangement for arriving at political decisions in which individuals acquire the power to decide by means of a competitive struggle for the people's vote."[6]

Democracy is thus conceived primarily in procedural terms; it is seen as a method of making decisions which insures efficiency in administration and policy making and yet requires some measure of responsiveness to popular opinion on the part of the ruling elites. The average citizen still has some measure of effective political power under this system, even though he does not initiate policy, because of his right to vote (if he chooses) in regularly scheduled elections. The political leaders, in an effort to gain support at the polls, will shape public policy to fit the citizens' desires. By anticipating public reaction the elite grants the citizenry a form of indirect access to public policy making, without the creation of any kind of formal institution and even in the absence of any direct communication. "A few citizens who are non-voters, and who for some reason have no influential contact with voters, have no indirect influence. Most citizens, however, possess a moderate degree of indirect influence, for elected officials keep the real or imagined preferences of constituents constantly in mind in deciding what policies to adopt or reject."[7] An ambiguity is created here because obviously leaders sometimes create opinions as well as respond to them, but since the leaders are constantly being challenged by rivals seeking to gain the allegiance of the masses it is assumed that the individual citizen will receive information from several conflicting sources, making it extremely difficult for any one group to "engineer consent" by manipulating public opinion. As Lipset puts it: "Representation is neither simply a means of political adjustment to social pressures nor an instrument of manipulation. It involves both functions, since the purpose of representation is to locate the combinations of relationships between parties and social bases which make possible the operation of efficient government."[8]

There has been extensive research and speculation about the prerequisites for a democratic system of this kind. There is general agreement that a well-developed social pluralism and an extensive system of voluntary groups or associations is needed along with a prevailing sense of psychological security, widespread education, and limited disparities of wealth. There must be no arbitrary barriers to political participation, and "enough people must participate in the governmental process so that political leaders compete for the support of a large and more or less representative cross section of the population."[9]

Elitist theory departs markedly from the classical tradition at this point. Traditionally it was assumed that the most important prerequisite for a stable democracy was general agreement among the politically active (those who vote) on certain fundamental policies and basic values, and widespread acceptance of democratic procedures and restraints on political activity. Political leaders would not violate the basic consensus, or "democratic mold," if they wished to be successful in gaining their objectives, because once these fundamental restraints were broken the otherwise passive public would become aroused and would organize against the offending leaders. Elitist theorists argue instead that agreement on democratic values among the "intervening structure of elites," the very elements which had been seen earlier as potential threats to democracy, is the main bulwark against a breakdown in constitutionalism. Writing in 1959 David Truman discards his notion of "potential groups," a variation of the traditional doctrine of consensus, and calls instead for a "concensus of elites," a determination on the part of the leaders of political parties, labor unions, trade associations and other voluntary associations to defend the fundamental procedures of democracy in order to protect their own positions and the basic structure of society itself from the threat of an irresponsible demagogue.[10] V. O. Key, in his *Public Opinion and the American Democracy,* concludes that "the critical element for the health of a democratic order consists in the beliefs, standards, and competence of those who constitute the influentials, the opinion-leaders, the political activists in the order." [11] Similarly, Robert Dahl concludes in his study of New Haven that the skillful, active political leaders in the system are the true democratic "legitimists."[12] Since democratic procedures regulate their conflicts and protect their privileged positions in the system the leaders can be counted on to defend the democratic creed even if a majority of the voters might prefer some other set of procedures.[13]

It has also been suggested by several elitist theorists that democracies have good reason to fear increased political participation. They argue that a successful (that is, stable) democratic system depends on widespread apathy and general political incompetence.[14] The ideal of democratic participation is thus transformed into a "noble lie" designed chiefly to insure a sense of responsibility among political leaders. As Lester Milbrath puts it: ". . . it is important to continue moral admonishment for citizens to become active in politics, not because we want or expect great masses of them to become active, but rather because the admonishment helps keep the system open and sustains a belief in the right of all to participate, which is an important norm governing the behavior of political elites."[15] If the uninformed masses participate in large numbers, democratic self-restraint will break down and peaceful competition among the elites, the central element in the elitist theory, will become impossible.

The principal aim of the critics whose views we are examining has been to make the theory of democracy more realistic, to bring it into closer correspondence with empirical reality. They are convinced that the classical theory does not account for "much of the real machinery"[16] by which the system operates, and they have expressed concern about the possible spread among Americans of either unwarranted anxiety or cynical disillusionment over the condition of democracy. But it is difficult to transform a utopian theory into a realistic account of political behavior without changing the theory's normative foundations. By revising the theory to bring it into closer correspondence with reality, the elitist theorists have transformed democracy from a radical into a conservative political doctrine, stripping away its distinctive emphasis on popular political activity so that it no longer serves as a set of ideals toward which society ought to be striving.[17]

The most distinctive feature, and the principal orienting value, of classical democratic theory was its emphasis on individual participation in the development of public policy. By taking part in the affairs of his society the citizen would gain in knowledge and understanding, develop a deeper sense of social responsibility, and broaden his perspective beyond the narrow confines of his private life. Although the classical theorists accepted the basic framework of Lockean democracy, with its emphasis on limited government, they were *not* primarily concerned with the *policies* which might be produced in a democracy; above all else they were concerned with *human development,* the opportunities which existed in political activity to realize the untapped potentials of men and to create the foundations of a genuine human community. In the words of John Stuart Mill: "... the most important point of excellence which any form of government can possess is to promote the virtue and intelligence of the people themselves. The first question in respect to any political institutions is how far they tend to foster in the members of the community the various desirable qualities, . . . moral, intellectual, and active."[18]

In the elitist version of the theory, however, emphasis has shifted to the needs and functions of the system as a whole; there is no longer a direct concern with human development. The central question is not how to design a political system which stimulates greater individual participation and enhances the moral development of its citizens, but how "to combine a substantial degree of popular participation with a system of power capable of governing *effectively* and *coherently.*[19]

The elitist theory allows the citizen only a passive role as an object of political activity; he exerts influence on policy making only by rendering judgments after the fact in national elections. The safety of contemporary democracy lies in the high-minded sense of responsibility of its leaders, the only elements of society who are actively striving to discover and implement the common good. The citizens are left to "judge a world they never made, and thus to become a genteel counterpart of the mobs which sporadically unseated aristocratic governments in eighteenth- and nineteenth-century Europe."[20]

The contemporary version of democratic theory has, it seems, lost much of the vital force, the radical thrust of the classical theory. The elitist theorists, in trying to develop a theory which takes account of the way the political system actually operates, have changed the principal orienting values of democracy. The heart of the classical theory was its justification of broad participation in the public affairs of the community; the aim was the production of citizens who were capable enough and responsible enough to play this role. The classical theory was not meant to describe any existing system of government; it was an outline, a set of prescriptions for the ideal polity which men should strive to create. The elitist theorists, in their quest for realism, have changed this distinctive prescriptive element in democratic theory; they have substituted stability and efficiency as the prime goals of democracy. If these revisions are accepted, the danger arises that in striving to develop more reliable explanations of political behavior, political scientists will also become sophisticated apologists for the existing political order. Robert Lane, in concluding his study of the political ideologies of fifteen "common men" in an Eastern city, observes that they lack a utopian vision, a well-defined sense of social justice that would allow them to stand in judgment on their society and its institutions.[21] To some degree, the "men of Eastport" share this disability with much of the American academic elite.

THE ELITIST THEORY AS A GUIDE FOR RESEARCH

The shortcomings of the elitist theory are not confined to its normative implications. Serious questions also arise concerning its descriptive accuracy and its utility as a guide to empirical research. The most unsatisfactory element in the theory is its concept of the passive, apolitical, common man who pays allegiance to his governors and to the sideshow of politics while remaining primarily concerned with his private life, evenings of television with his family, or the demands of his job. Occasionally, when the average citizen finds his primary goals threatened by the actions or inactions of government, he may strive vigorously to influence the course of public policy, but *"homo civicus"* as Dahl calls him, "is not, by nature, a political animal."[22]

It was the acceptance of this concept that led the elitist theorists to reject the traditional notion of consensus. It became implausible to argue that the citizenry is watchful and jealous of the great democratic values while at the same time suggesting that they are uninvolved, uninformed, and apathetic. Widespread apathy also is said to contribute to democratic stability by insuring that the disagreements that arise during campaigns and elections will not involve large numbers of people or plunge the society into violent disorders or civil war.

No one can deny that there is widespread political apathy among many sectors of the American public. But it is important to ask why this is so and not simply to explain how this phenomenon contributes to the smooth functioning of the system. Of course, the citizens' passivity might stem from their satisfaction with the operation of the political system, and thus they would naturally become aroused only if they perceived a threat to the system. Dahl, for one, argues that the political system operates largely through "inertia," tradition, or habitual responses. It remains stable because only a few "key" issues are the objects of controversy at any one time, the rest of public policy having been settled and established in past controversies which are now all but forgotten. Similarly, Nelson Polsby argues that it is fallacious to assume that the quiescent citizens in a community, especially those in the lower income groups, have grievances unless they actually express them. To do so is to arbitrarily assign "upper- and middle-class values to all actors in the community."[23]

But it is hard to believe, in these days of protest demonstrations, of Black Muslins and the Deacons of Defense and Justice, that the mood of cynical apathy toward politics which affects so many American Negroes is an indication of their satisfaction with the political system and with the weak, essentially meaningless alternatives it usually presents to them. To assume that apathy is a sign of satisfaction in this case is to overlook the tragic history of the Negroes in America and the system of violent repression long used to deny them any entrance into the regular channels of democratic decision-making.

Students of race relations have concluded that hostile attitudes toward a racial group do not necessarily lead to hostile actions, and amicable feelings do not ensure amicable actions. Instead, "it is the social demands of the situation, particularly when supported by accepted authority figures, which are the effective determinants of individual action. . . ."[24] This insight might apply to other areas besides race relations. It suggests that society's political culture, the general perceptions about the nature of authority and the prevailing expectations of significant reference groups, might be a major influence on the political behavior of the average citizen regardless of his own feelings of satisfaction or hostility. There have been sizable shifts in rates of political participation throughout American history which suggests that these rates are not rigidly determined. A recent analysis indicates that rates of voter participation are now *lower* than they were in the nineteenth century even though the population is now much better educated and the facilities for communication much better developed.[25] Other studies indicate that there are marked differences in the political milieu of towns and cities which lead citizens of one area to exhibit much more cynicism and distrust of the political system than others.[26] Although the studies showed no corresponding changes in feelings of political competence, cynical attitudes might inhibit many forms of participation and thus induce apathy.

Political apathy obviously has many sources. It may stem from feelings of personal inadequacy, from a fear of endangering important personal relationships, or from a lack of interest in the issues; but it may also have its roots in the society's institutional structure, in the weakness or absence of group stimulation or support, in the positive opposition of elements within the political system to wider participation; in the absence, in other words, of appropriate spurs to action or the presence of tangible deterrents.[27] Before the causes of apathy can be established with confidence much more attention must be directed to the role of the mass media. How are the perceptions of individual citizens affected by the version of reality they receive, either directly or indirectly, from television, the national wire services, and the public schools[28]—and how do these perceptions affect their motivations? Political scientists have also largely neglected to study the use of both legitimate and illegitimate sanctions and private intimidation to gain political ends. How do the activities of the police,[29] social workers, or elements of organized crime affect the desires and the opportunities available for individual political participation?

Certainly the apparent calm of American politics is not matched by our general social life, which is marked by high crime rates, numerous fads and crazes, and much intergroup tension.[30] One recent study showed that during the civil rights protests in Atlanta, Georgia, and Cambridge, Maryland, crime rates in the Negro communities dropped substantially.[31] A finding of this kind suggests that there is some connection between these two realms of social conflict and that both may serve as outlets for individual distress and frustration. High crime (or suicide) rates and low rates of voting may very well be related; the former may represent "leakage" from the political system.[32]

Once we admit that the society is not based on a widespread consensus, we must look at our loosely organized, decentralized political parties in a different light. It may be that the parties have developed in this way precisely because no broad consensus exists. In a fragmented society which contains numerous geographic, religious, and racial conflicts, the successful politician has been the man adept at negotiation and bargaining, the man best able to play these numerous animosities off against each other and thereby build *ad hoc* coalitions of support for specific programs. Success at this delicate business of coalition building depends on achieving some basis for communication among the leaders of otherwise antagonistic groups and finding a formula for compromise. To create these circumstances sharp conflicts must be avoided and highly controversial, potentially explosive issues shunned. Controversy is shifted to other issues or the public authorities simply refuse to deal with the question, claiming that they have no legitimate jurisdiction in the case or burying it quietly in some committee room or bureaucratic pigeonhole.[33]

In other words, one of the chief characteristics of our political system has been its success in suppressing and controlling internal conflict. But the avoidance of conflict, the suppression of strife, is *not* necessarily the creation of satisfaction or consensus. The citizens may remain quiescent, the political system might retain its stability, but significant differences of opinion remain, numerous conflicts are unresolved, and many desires go unfulfilled. The frustrations resulting from such deprivations can create conflict in other, nonpolitical realms. Fads, religious revivals, or wild, anomic riots such as those which occurred in the Negro ghettos of several large American cities during the summers of 1964 and 1965, phenomena not directly related to the achievement of any clearly conceived political goals, may be touched off by unresolved tensions left untended by the society's political leaders.

The American political system is highly complex, with conflicting jurisdictions and numerous checks and balances. A large commitment in time and energy must be made, even by a well-educated citizen, to keep informed of the issues and personalities in all levels of government. Most citizens are not able or willing to pay this kind of cost to gain the information necessary for effective political participation. This may be especially true in a political system in which weak or unclear alternatives are usually presented to the electorate. For most citizens the world of politics is remote, bewildering, and meaningless, having no direct relation to daily concerns about jobs or family life. Many citizens have desires or frustrations with which public agencies might be expected to deal, but they usually remain unaware of possible solutions to their problems in the public sphere. This group within our political system are citizens only from the legal point of view. If a high degree of social solidarity and sense of community are necessary for true democratic participation, then these marginal men are not really citizens of the state. The polity has not been extended to include them.[34]

For the elitist theorist widespread apathy is merely a fact of political life, something to be anticipated, a prerequisite for democratic stability. But for the classical democrat political apathy is an object of intense concern because the overriding moral purpose of the classical theory is to expand the boundaries of the political community and build the foundations for human understanding through participation by the citizens in the affairs of their government.

LEADERS AND FOLLOWERS

While most elitist theorists are agreed in conceiving of the average citizen as politically passive and uncreative, there seems to be a difference of opinion (or at least of emphasis) over the likelihood of some irrational, antidemocratic outburst from the society's common men. Dahl does not dwell on this possibility. He seemingly conceives of *homo civicus,* the average citizen, as a man who consciously chooses to avoid politics and to devote himself to the pleasures and problems of his job and family:

> Typically, as a source of direct gratifications political activity will appear to *homo civicus* as less attractive than a host of other activities; and, as a strategy to achieve his gratifications indirectly political action will seem considerably less efficient than working at his job, earning more money, taking out insurance, joining a club, planning a vacation, moving to another neighborhood or city, or coping with an uncertain future in manifold other ways.[35]

Lipset, on the other hand, seems much more concerned with the danger that the common man might suddenly enter the political system, smashing democratic institutions in the process, as part of an irrational, authoritarian political force. He sees "profoundly antidemocratic tendencies in lower class groups,"[36] and he has been frequently concerned in his work with Hitler, McCarthy, and other demagogic leaders who have led antidemocratic mass movements.

Although there are obviously some important differences of opinion and emphasis concerning the political capacities of average citizens and the relative security of democratic institutions, the elitist theorists agree on the crucial importance of leadership in insuring both the safety and viability of representative government. This set of basic assumptions serves as a foundation for their explanation of change and innovation in American politics, a process in which they feel creative leadership plays the central role.

Running throughout the work of these writers is a vision of the "professional" politician as hero, much as he is pictured in Max Weber's essay, "Politics as a Vocation." Dahl's Mayor Lee, Edward Banfield's Mayor Daley, Richard Neustadt's ideal occupant of the White House all possess great skill and drive and are engaged in the delicate art of persuasion and coalition building. They are actively moving the society forward toward their own goals, according to their own special vision. All of them possess the pre-eminent qualities of Weber's ideal-type politician: "passion, a feeling of responsibility, and a sense of proportion."[37] As in Schumpeter's analysis of capitalism, the primary source of change and innovation in the political system is the "political entrepreneur"; only such a leader can break through the inherent conservatism of organizations and shake the masses from their habitual passivity.

It is obvious that political leaders (especially chief executives) have played a very important role in American politics, but it is also clear that the American system's large degree of internal bargaining, the lack of many strong hierarchical controls and its numerous checks and balances, both constitutional and political, place powerful constraints on the behavior of political executives. American presidents, governors, and mayors usually find themselves caught in a web of cross pressures which prevent them from making bold departures in policy or firmly attaching themselves to either side of a controversy. The agenda of controversy, the list of questions which are recognized by the active participants in politics as legitimate subjects of attention and concern, is very hard to change.

Just as it can be argued that the common citizens have a form of indirect influence, so it can also be argued that the top leaders of other institutions in the society, such as the business community, possess indirect influence as well. As Banfield suggests in his study of Chicago, the top business leaders have great potential power: "if the twenty or thirty wealthiest men in Chicago acted as one and put all their wealth into the fight, they could easily destroy or capture the machine."[38] The skillful politician, following Carl Friedrich's "rule of anticipated reactions,"[39] is unlikely to make proposals which would unite the business community against him. The aspiring politician learns early in his career, by absorbing the folklore which circulates among the politically active, which issues can and cannot be exploited successfully. It is this constellation of influences and anticipated reactions, "the peculiar mobilization of bias" in the community, fortified by a general consensus of elites, that determines the agenda of controversy.[40] The American political system, above all others, seems to be especially designed to frustrate the creative leader.

But as rigid and inflexible as it is, the political system does produce new policies; new programs and schemes are approved; even basic procedural changes are made from time to time. Of course, each major shift in public policy has a great many causes. The elitist theory of democracy looks for the principal source of innovation in the competition among rival leaders and the clever maneuvering of political entrepreneurs, which is, in its view, the most distinctive aspect of a democratic system. Because so many political scientists have worn the theoretical blinders of the elitist theory, however, we have overlooked the importance of broadly based social movements, arising from the public at large, as powerful agents of innovation and change:

The primary concerns of the elitist theorists have been the maintenance of democratic stability, the preservation of democratic stability, the preservation of democratic procedures, and the creation of machinery which would produce efficient administration and coherent public policies. With these goals in mind, social movements (if they have been studied at all) have usually been pictured as threats to democracy, as manifestations of "political extremism." Lipset asserts that such movements typically appeal to the "disgruntled and the psychologically homeless, to the personal failures, the socially isolated, the economically insecure, the uneducated, unsophisticated, and authoritarian persons at every level of the society."[41] Movements of this kind throw the political system out of gear and disrupt the mechanisms designed to maintain due process;

if the elites were overwhelmed by such forces, democracy would be destroyed. This narrow, antagonistic view of social movements stems from the elitist theorists' suspicion of the political capacities of the common citizens,[42] their fear of instability, and their failure to recognize the elements of rigidity and constraint existing in the political system. But if one holds that view and at the same time recognizes the tendency of the prevailing political system to frustrate strong leaders, it becomes difficult to explain how significant innovations in public policy, such as the social security system, the Wagner Act, the Subversive Activities Control Act of 1950, or the Civil Rights Bill of 1964, ever came about.

During the last century American society has spawned numerous social movements, some of which have made extensive demands on the political system, while others have been highly esoteric, mystical, and apolitical. These movements arise because some form of social dislocation or widespread sense of frustration exists within the society. But dissatisfaction alone is not a sufficient cause; it must be coupled with the necessary resources and the existence of potential leadership which can motivate a group to take action designed to change the offending circumstances.[43] Often such movements erupt along the margins of the political system, and they sometimes serve the purpose of encouraging political and social mobilization, of widening the boundaries of the polity.[44] Through movements such as the Negroes' drive for civil rights, or the Midwestern farmers' crusade for fair prices in the 1890's, or the Ku Klux Klan, or the "radical right" movements of the 1960's, *"prepolitical* people who have not yet found, or only begun to find, a specific language in which to express their aspirations about the world"[45] are given new orientation, confidence, knowledge, sources of information, and leadership.

Social movements also serve, in Rudolf Heberle's words, as the "creators and carriers of public opinion."[46] By confronting the political authorities, or by locking themselves in peaceful—or violent[47]—conflict with some other element of the society, social movements provoke trials of strength between contending forces or ideas. Those trials of economic, political, or moral strength take place in the court of public opinion and sometimes place enormous strain on democratic institutions and even the social fabric itself. But through such trials, as tumultuous as they may sometimes be, the agenda of controversy, the list of acceptable, "key" issues may be changed. In an effort to conciliate and mediate, the political leaders fashion new legislation, create unique regulatory bodies, and strive to establish channels of communication and accommodation among the combatants.

Of course, members of the political elite may respond to the movement by resisting it, driving it underground, or destroying it; they may try to co-opt the movement's leaders by granting them privileges or by accepting parts of its program, or even by making the leaders part of the established elite; they may surrender to the movement, losing control of their offices in the political system in the process. The nature of the political leader's response is probably a prime determinant of the tactics the movement will adopt, the kind of leadership that arises within it, and the ideological appeals it develops. Other factors might determine the response of the leadership, such as the existence of competing social movements with conflicting demands, the resources available to the political leaders to satisfy the demands of the movement, the social status of the participants in the movement, the presence of competing sets of leaders claiming to represent the same movement, and many other elements peculiar to each particular situation. In this process social movements may be highly disruptive and some institutions may be completely destroyed; the story does not always have a happy ending. But one major consequence (function, if you will) of social movements is to break society's log jams, to prevent ossification in the political system, to prompt and justify major innovations in social policy and economic organization.[48]

This relationship of challenge and response between the established political system and social movements has gone without much systematic study by political scientists. Sociologists have been concerned with social movements, but they have directed most of their attention to the causes of the movements, their "natural history," and the relationship between leaders and followers within them.[49] Historians have produced many case studies of social movements but little in the way of systematic explanation.[50] This would seem to be a fruitful area for investigation by political scientists. But this research is not likely to appear unless we revise our concept of the masses as politically inert, apathetic, and bound by habitual responses. We must also shift our emphasis from theories which conceive of the "social structure in terms of a functionally integrated system held in equilibrium by certain patterned and recurrent processes" to theories which place greater emphasis on the role of coercion and constraint in the political system and which concentrate on the influences within society which produce "the forces that maintain it in an unending process of change."[51] The greatest contribution of Marx to the understanding of society was his realization that internal conflict is a major source of change and innovation. One need not accept his metaphysical assumptions to appreciate this important insight.

CONCLUSION

In a society undergoing massive social change, fresh theoretical perspectives are essential. Political theorists are charged with the responsibility of constantly reformulating the dogmas of the past so that democratic theory remains relevant to the stormy realities of twentieth century American society with its sprawling urban centers, its innumerable social conflicts, and its enormous bureaucratic hierarchies.

In restating the classical theory, however, contemporary political scientists have stripped democracy of much of its radical *élan* and have diluted its utopian vision, thus rendering it inadequate as a guide to the future. The elitist theorists generally accept the prevailing distribution of status in the society (with exceptions usually made for the American

Negro) and find it "not only compatible with political freedom but even ... a condition of it."[52] They place great emphasis on the limitations of the average citizen and are suspicious of schemes which might encourage greater participation in public affairs. Accordingly, they put their trust in the wisdom and energy of an active, responsible elite.

Besides these normative shortcomings the elitist theory has served as an inadequate guide to empirical research, providing an unconvincing explanation of widespread political apathy in American society and leading political scientists to ignore manifestations of discontent not directly related to the political system. Few studies have been conducted of the use of force, or informal, illegitimate coercion in the American political system, and little attention has been directed to the great social movements which have marked American society in the last one hundred years.

If political science is to be relevant to society's pressing needs and urgent problems, professional students of politics must broaden their perspectives and become aware of new problems which are in need of scientific investigation. They must examine the norms that guide their efforts and guard against the danger of uncritically accepting the values of the going system in the name of scientific objectivity. Political scientists must strive for heightened awareness and self-knowledge; they must avoid rigid presumptions which diminish their vision, destroy their capacities for criticism, and blind them to some of the most significant social and political developments of our time.

NOTES

1. For discussions of the meaning of the classical theory of democracy see: George Sabine, "The Two Democratic Traditions," *The Philosophical Review,* 61 (1952), 451–474; and his *A History of Political Theory* (New York, 1958), especially chs. 31 and 32. Also see J. Roland Pennock, *Liberal Democracy: Its Merits and Prospects* (New York, 1950); and Sheldon Wolin, *Politics and Vision* (Boston, 1960), especially chs. 9 and 10.

2. Criticism of the descriptive accuracy of the classical theory has been widespread in recent years. The best statement of the basic objections usually made is Joseph Schumpeter, *Capitalism, Socialism and Democracy* (New York, 1942), part IV. See also Bernard Berelson *et al.*, *Voting* (Chicago, 1954), ch. 14; articles by Louis Hartz and Samuel Beer in W. N. Chambers and R. H. Salisbury (eds.), *Democracy in the Mid-20th Century* (St. Louis, 1960); Seymour Martin Lipset, *Political Man* (New York, 1960); Robert Dahl, *A Preface to Democratic Theory* (Chicago, 1956), and *Who Governs?* (New Haven, 1961), especially pp. 223–325; V. O. Key, *Public Opinion and American Democracy* (New York, 1961), especially part VI; Lester W. Milbrath, *Political Participation* (Chicago, 1965), especially ch. 6; and for a general summary of the position, Henry Mayo, *An Introduction to Democratic Theory* (New York, 1960).

3. Introduction by Lipset to the Collier Books paperback edition of Robert Michel's *Political Parties* (New York, 1962), p. 33.

4. The phrase is Dahl's in *Who Governs?*, p. 227.

5. *Ibid.*, p. 225.

6. Schumpeter, *op. cit.*, p. 269.

7. Dahl, *Who Governs?*, p. 164.

8. Lipset, Introduction to Michels, *op. cit.*, p. 34.

9. Robert Dahl and Charles Lindblom, *Politics, Economics and Welfare* (New York, 1953), p. 309.

10. David Truman, "The American System in Crisis," *Political Science Quarterly* (December, 1959), pp. 481–497. See also a perceptive critique of Truman's change of attitude in Peter Bachrach, "Elite Consensus and Democracy," *The Journal of Politics*, 24 (1962), 439–452.

11. Key, *op. cit.*, p. 558. See also Key's "Public Opinion and the Decay of Democracy," *The Virginia Quarterly Review*, 37 (1961), 481–494.

12. Dahl's position on this issue seems to have undergone a transformation somewhat similar to Truman's. Compare Dahl and Lindblom, *op. cit.*, ch. 11 with Dahl, *Who Governs?*, books IV, V, VI.

13. Dahl, *Who Governs?*, pp. 311–325. It is important to note that these conclusions about the crucial function of an elite consensus in democracy were based on little empirical evidence. Truman, Key, and Dahl seem to rely most heavily on Samuel Stouffer, *Communism, Conformity, and Civil Liberties* (New York, 1955), a study based on national opinion surveys which was concerned with only one issue (McCarthyism) and did not investigate the relationship between the expressed opinions of its subjects and their behavior under stress; and James Prothro and Charles Grigg, "Fundamental Principles of Democracy: Bases of Agreement and Disagreement," *Journal of Politics*, 22 (1960), 276–294, a study of attitudes in two small cities. More recently, however, Herbert McClosky has produced more convincing data in his "Consensus and Ideology in American Politics," *American Political Science Review*, 58 (1964), 361–382. On p. 377 McClosky concludes that widespread agreement on procedural norms is not a prerequisite to the success of a democratic system: "Consensus may strengthen democratic viability, but its absence in an otherwise stable society need not be fatal, or even

particularly damaging." McClosky's conclusions are called into question by data presented by Samuel Eldersveld, *Political Parties: A Behavioral Analysis* (Chicago, 1964), pp. 183–219; and Edmond Constantini, "Intraparty Attitude Conflict: Democratic Party Leadership in California," *Western Political Quarterly*, 16 (1963), 956–972.

14. See Bernard Berelson *et al., op. cit.,* ch. 14; Lipset, *op. cit.,* pp. 14–16; W. H. Morris-Jones, "In Defense of Apathy," *Political Studies,* II (1954), 25–37.
15. Milbrath, *op. cit.,* p. 152.
16. Louis Hartz, "Democracy: Image and Reality," in Chambers and Salisbury (eds.), *op. cit.,* p. 26.
17. Several articles have recently appeared which attack the elitist theory on normative grounds. The best and most insightful is Lane Davis, "The Cost of Realism: Contemporary Restatements of Democracy," *Western Political Quarterly,* 17 (1964), 37–46. Also see: Graeme Duncan and Steven Lukes, "The New Democracy," *Political Studies,* 11 (1963), 156–177; Steven W. Rousseas and James Farganis, "American Politics and the End of Ideology," *British Journal of Sociology,* 14 (1963), 347–360; and Christian Bay, "Politics and Pseudopolitics," *American Political Science Review,* 59 (1965), 39–51. The subject is also treated in: Henry Kariel, *The Decline of American Pluralism* (Stanford, 1961), chs. 9 and 11; T. B. Bottomore, *Elites and Society* (London, 1964), pp. 108–110; Robert Presthus, *Men at the Top* (New York, 1964), pp. 3–47; and Robert Agger, Daniel Goldrich, and Bert Swanson, *The Rulers and the Ruled* (New York), 1964, pp. 93–99, 524–532. For an insightful critique of the work of Dahl and Mills, conceived of as opposing ideological positions see: William E. Connolly, "Responsible Political Ideology: Implications of the Sociology of Knowledge for Political Inquiry" (unpublished doctoral dissertation, University of Michigan, 1965), pp. 18–39. This section of this article depends heavily on Lane Davis' analysis.
18. John Stuart Mill, *Considerations on Representative Government* (New York, 1862), pp. 39–40.
19. Samuel Beer, "New Structures of Democracy: Britain and America," in Chambers and Salisbury (eds.), *op. cit.,* p. 46.
20. Davis, *op. cit.,* p. 45.
21. Robert Lane, *Political Ideology* (New York, 1962), p. 475. See also Donald Stokes' comments on the same topic in "Popular Evaluations of Government: An Empirical Assessment," in Harlan Cleveland and Harold Lasswell (eds.), *Ethics and Bigness* (Published by the Conference on Science, Philosophy and Religion in their relation to the Democratic Way of Life, 1962), p. 72.
22. Dahl, *Who Governs?,* p. 225.
23. Nelson Polsby, *Community Power and Political Theory* (New Haven, 1963), p. 117.
24. Herbert Blumer, "Recent research [on race relations in the] United States of America," *International Social Science Bulletin* (UNESCO), 10 (1958), p. 432. Similar arguments concerning the relationship of beliefs and action can be found in J. D. Lohman and D. C. Reitzes, "Deliberately Organized Groups and Racial Behavior," *American Sociological Review,* 19 (1954), 342–344; and in Earl

Raab (ed.), *American Race Relations Today* (Garden City, 1962).

25. Walter Dean Burnham, "The Changing Shape of the American Political Universe," APSR, 59 (1965), 7–28.

26. Robert Agger, Marshall Goldstein, and Stanley Pearl, "Political Cynicism: Measurement and Meaning," *The Journal of Politics*, 23 (1961), 477–506; and Edgar Litt, "Political Cynicism and Political Futility," *The Journal of Politics*, 25 (1963), 312–323.

27. For a brief survey of findings on this subject, see Milbrath, *op. cit.;* and for a clear, brief summary, see: Morris Rosenburg, "Some Determinants of Political Apathy," *Public Opinion Quarterly*, 18 (1954–55), 349–366. Also see David Apter (ed.), *Ideology and Discontent* (New York, 1964), especially chapters by Converse and Wolfinger *et al.*

28. A major study of the influence of secondary schools on political attitudes is underway at the University of Michigan under the direction of M. Kent Jennings.

29. An extensive investigation of the role of the police and the courts in city politics is being conducted at Harvard University by James Q. Wilson.

30. It is very difficult to compare crime rates or other indications of social disorganization in the United States with those in other countries. For a discussion of some of the difficulties see: UNESCO 1963 *Report on the World Social Situation* (New York, 1963).

31. Fredric Solomon, Walter L. Walker, Garrett O'Connor, and Jacob Fishman, "Civil Rights Activity and Reduction of Crime Among Negroes," *Archives of General Psychiatry*, 12 (March, 1965), 227–236.

32. For an excellent study of the Black Muslims which portrays the movement as a nonpolitical outlet for the frustration and bitterness felt by many American Negroes see the study by an African scholar: E. V. Essien-Udom, *Black Nationalism: A Search for an Identity in America* (Chicago, 1962).

33. Herbert Agar makes a similar analysis and argues for the retention of the system in *The Price of Union* (Boston, 1950). On p. 689 he states: "The lesson which Americans learned [from the Civil War] was useful: in a large federal nation, when a problem is passionately felt, and is discussed in terms of morals, each party may divide within itself, against itself. And if the parties divide, the nation may divide; for the parties, with their enjoyable pursuit of power, are a unifying influence. Wise men, therefore, may seek to dodge such problems as long as possible. And the easiest way to dodge them is for both parties to take both sides."

34. For a study of several important factors affecting the degree of participation in American politics see: E. E. Schattschneider, *The Semi-Sovereign People* (New York, 1960), especially chs. 5 and 6.

35. Dahl, *Who Governs?*, p. 224.

36. Lipset, *op. cit.*, p. 121.

37. Hans Gerth and C. Wright Mills (eds.), *From Max Weber: Essays in Sociology* (New York, 1946), p. 115.

38. Edward Banfield, *Political Influence* (New York, 1961), p. 290.

39. Carl Friedrich, *Constitutional Government and Politics* (New York, 1939), pp. 17–18.

40. This point is made persuasively by Peter Bachrach and Morton

Baratz, "The Two Faces of Power," *American Political Science Review*, 56 (1952), 947–952. Also see their "Decisions and Non-decisions: An Analytical Framework," *American Political Science Review*, 57 (1963), 632–642; and Thomas J. Anton, "Power, Pluralism and Local Politics," *Administrative Quarterly*, 7 (1963), 425–457.

41. Lipset, *op. cit.*, p. 178.

42. Ruth Searles and J. Allen Williams, in a study of Negro students who took part in the sit-in demonstrations, found no evidence that they were authoritarian or posed threats to democracy. "Far from being alienated, the students appear to be committed to the society and its middle class leaders": "Negro College Students' Participation in Sit-ins," *Social Forces*, 40 (1962), 219. For other studies of this particular social movement see: Robert Coles, "Social Struggle and Weariness," *Psychiatry*, 27 (1964), 305–315; and three articles by Fredric Solomon and Jacob Fishman: "Perspectives on the Student Sit-in Movement," *American Journal of Ortho-psychiatry*, 33 (1963), 872–882; "Action and Identity Formation in the First Student Sit-in Demonstration," *Journal of Social Issues*, 20 (1964), 36–45; and "Psychosocial Meaning of Nonviolence in Student Civil Rights Activities," *Psychiatry*, 27 (1964), 91–99. Also see the October 1964 issue of *The Journal of Social Issues*, entitled "Youth and Social Action," edited by Fredric Solomon and Jacob Fishman; and Jack L. Walker, "Protest and Negotiation: A Case Study of Negro Leaders in Atlanta, Georgia," *Midwest Journal of Political Science*, 7 (1963), 99–124.

43. Sociologists usually study social movements under the rubric of collective behavior. For general treatments see: Herbert Blumer, "Collective Behavior" in J. B. Gittler (ed.), *Review of Sociology* (New York, 1957); Rudolph Heberle, *Social Movements* (New York, 1951); Lewis Killian, "Social Movements" in Robert Faris (ed.), *Handbook of Modern Sociology* (Chicago, 1964); Charles King, *Social Movements in the United States* (New York, 1956); Karl Lang and Gladys Lang, *Collective Dynamics* (New York, 1961); Neil Smelser, *Theory of Collective Behavior* (New York, 1963); Ralph Turner and Lewis Killian, *Collective Behavior* (Englewood Cliffs, N.J., 1957). For a brief historical sketch of some American social movements see: Thomas Greer, *American Social Reform Movements: Their Pattern Since 1865* (Englewood Cliffs, N. J., 1946).

44. For a book which investigates social movements which have served this function among Italian peasants see: E. J. Hobsbawn, *Primitive Rebels* (Manchester, 1959). See also: Vittorio Lanternari, *The Religions of the Oppressed* (New York, 1963) for a study of the relationship of Messianic Cults and revolutionary movements on five continents; and George Rude, *The Crowd in History* (New York, 1964) for a study of popular uprisings in England and France from 1730–1848.

45. Hobsbawn, *op. cit.*, p. 2.

46. Heberle, *op. cit.*, pp. 417–418.

47. American political scientists have not been sufficiently concerned with the role of violence in the governmental process. Among all the articles published in *The American Political Science Review* be-

tween 1906 and 1963, there was only one whose title contained the word "violence," only one with the word "coercive" (it concerned India), and none with the word "force." During the same period there were forty-nine articles on governmental reorganization and twenty-four on civil service reform. See Kenneth Janda (ed.), *Cumulative Index to The American Political Science Review* (Evanston, 1964). Efforts to retrieve this situation have begun in Harry Eckstein (ed.), *Internal War* (New York, 1964).

48. Lewis Coser has discussed the role of conflict in provoking social change in his *The Functions of Social Conflict* (Glencoe, 1956); and in his "Social Conflict and the Theory of Social Change," *British Journal of Sociology,* 9 (1957), 197–207. See also Irving Louis Horowitz, "Consensus, Conflict and Cooperation: A Sociological Inventory," *Social Forces,* 41 (1962), 177–188.

49. For an insightful and stimulating example, see Joseph Gusfield, *Symbolic Crusade* (Urbana, 1963), which makes an excellent analysis of the causes of the Temperance movement and changes in its leadership but makes only brief mention of the movement's impact on the government and the responses of political leaders to its efforts.

50. John Higham is somewhat of an exception of this generalization. See his *Strangers in the Land: Patterns of American Nativism 1860–1925* (New York, 1963). Also see his "Another Look at Nativism," *Catholic Historical Review,* 44 (1958), 147–158; and his "The Cult of the 'American Consensus': Homogenizing Our History," *Commentary* (February, 1959), p. 159.

51. Ralf Dahrendorf, *Class and Class Conflict in Industrial Society* (Stanford, 1959), p. 159.

52. Sabine, "The Two Democratic Traditions," *op. cit.,* p. 459.

5. Further Reflections on "The Elitist Theory of Democracy"

ROBERT DAHL

An interest in the roles, functions, contributions, and dangers of leadership in popular regimes is not, of course, new among observers of political life. This has, in fact, been an ancient and enduring interest of political theorists. It is possible, however, to distinguish—at least in a rough way—two different streams of thought: one consisting of writers sympathetic to popular rule, the other consisting of anti-democratic writers.

It has always been obvious to practical and theoretical observers alike that even where leaders are chosen by the people, they might convert a democracy into an oligarchy or a despotism. From ancient times, as everyone knows, anti-democratic writers have contended that popular governments were unlikely to provide leaders with wisdom and virtue, and insisted

From *The American Political Science Review,* 60 (1966), 296–305. Reprinted by permission of the author and publisher.

on the natural affinity between the people and the despot. These ancient challenges by anti-democratic writers were, I think, made more formidable in the course of the last hundred years by critics—sometimes ex-democrats turned authoritarian when their Utopian hopes encountered the ugly realities of political life—who, like Pareto, Michels, and Mosca, contended that popular rule is not only undesirable but also, as they tried to show, *impossible*. The failure of popular regimes to emerge, or, if they did emerge, to survive, in Russia, Italy, Germany, and Spain could not be met merely by frequent assertions of democratic rhetoric.

Fortunately, alongside this stream of anti-democratic thought and experience there has always been the other. Aware both of their critics and of the real life problems of popular rule, writers sympathetic to democracy have emphasized the need for wisdom, virtue, and self-restraint not only among the general body of citizens but among leaders as well. Thus Aristotle gave his attention to the problems of leadership in popular orders at a number of points in the *Politics*.[1] Machiavelli, a tough-minded republican who knew from direct observation of Renaissance Europe the despotic propensities of political leaders, was fully aware of the dangers to popular rule generated by the need for and existence of leadership, but his solutions were not always enormously helpful—e.g., that every well-ordered republic should elect a succession of virtuous rulers (*principi*).[2] Although in the *Discourses* he did not elaborate on the problem of leadership in republics, his scattered observations show that he regarded the problem as significant and serious.[3]

Nor did Rousseau neglect the problem. In fact, it was the impossibility of arriving at all the conditions necessary for direct democracy, including the impossibility of keeping the people constantly assembled in order to decide public affairs, that led Rousseau to conclude that "democracy," in his sense, had never existed and never would. "If there were a people of gods, they would govern themselves democratically. A government so perfect is not suited to men."[4] Rousseau, no less than Plato, asserted that the best and most natural order is one in which the wisest govern the multitude, provided that the wisest govern for the benefit of the many and not for their own profit.[5]

Although John Stuart Mill emphasized the benefits to personal growth derived from political participation, as an admirer of Mill's like Professor Walker is surely aware, Mill did not advocate *equal* power: "Though every one ought to have a voice—that every one should have an equal voice is a totally different proposition. . . . If, with equal virtue, one [person] is superior to the other in knowledge and intelligence—or if, with equal intelligence, one excels the other in virtue—the opinion, the judgment, of the higher moral or intellectual being is worth more than that of the inferior: and if the institutions of the country virtually assert that they are of the same value, they assert a thing which is not."[6]

One could go on citing other writers generally sympathetic to democracy or representative government, but I hope there is no need. The point is not that I or Professor Walker must agree with their analysis, their solutions, or their descriptions. The point is that writers from the earliest times have understood that popular regimes, like other regimes, would inevitably have leaders—that is to say, men of more authority, and very likely more power and influence, than ordinary citizens. What kinds of leaders will—or should—the people elect? No doubt they should choose men of virtue and wisdom, but will they? How is this to be insured? What will happen if, as may be the case from time to time, they fail? These and similar concerns are ancient; the writers Professor Walker cites as "elitists" did not discover these questions: they sought to answer them in the light of modern experience.

I imagine that the heterogeneous collection of writers whose attention to the problems of leadership in popular orders stirs Professor Walker to regard them as "elitists" were all familiar with these two streams of thought and experience, the democratic and the anti-democratic. But they were also responding to the state of the debate as it seemed to stand around the middle of this century: for both recent history and recent theory had posed an extraordinarily sharp challenge to the validity of widely prevailing assumptions about popular government.

And unfortunately, despite several thousand years of attention given to the problems of leadership by theorists sympathetic with popular rule, the analysis of leadership in popular orders was unsystematic, incomplete, and based almost entirely on premodern experience. Although not all . . . will agree, and Professor Walker himself may not, it does not seem to me, nor I think to many other political scientists, that the questions raised in this century about leadership in democracies can be met satisfactorily by citing Aristotle, Machiavelli, Rousseau, Mill, or indeed any other theorist deprived of the opportunity to analyze the unfolding experience during the past half century or so with popular government in large, industrial, urbanized nation-states.

I

A number of writers committed to the success of popular regimes have therefore tried to examine the ancient problem of leadership, citizenship, and democracy by directly confronting recent experience. Had Professor Walker been content to make this point, no one, I am sure, would have found much to dispute in his essay—nor, for that matter, much of interest. What he has done, however, is something else: he has tried to reduce a variety of these recent efforts to a single body of doctrine.

Now any attempt to compress the views of many different writers to a simple statement is, I suppose, almost bound to distort their views, perhaps in quite important ways. In outlining what he has chosen to call "the elitist theory of democracy,"[7] Professor Walker has constructed a paradigm that his intended victims will all, I feel sure, regard as a caricature. Like every good caricature, it combines verisimilitude with exaggeration and distortion.

(1) It is an ancient academic game to create a "school" by asserting that it exists. But it is misleading to speak of "the" elitist theory of democracy as if such an entity existed. At various places the following writers in addition to myself seem to be construed as advocates of "*the* elitist theory": Beer, Berelson, Hartz, Lipset, Key, Mayo, Milbrath, McClosky, Morris-Jones, Polsby, Schumpeter, Truman, and somewhat strangely, since he is cited in the first footnote as an authority on the classical meaning of democracy, Sabine. I am puzzled as to what doctrine these writers are supposed to share—other than a belief in the desirability of representative government. I have tested the list against several criteria, each of which leads to absurdities. Is the common doctrime of these writers an emphasis on the empirical proposition that leaders do, as a matter of fact, have great weight in large, modern representative systems? If so, are there any students of modern politics who deny the proposition?[8] I would offer as further candidates for the list of proponents of "*the* elitist theory of democracy": Jefferson, Lincoln, Marx, Lenin, Mosca, Pareto, Michels, C. Wright Mills, and Professor Walker himself, since he has stressed as forcefully as most of his "elitist" writers the weight of leadership in "democracies." Isn't this too mixed a bag to be useful?

Is, then, the school of thought Professor Walker wishes to identify those writers who emphasize that in representative systems on the scale of the nation-state it is desirable to have leaders committed to democratic norms? If so, then the criterion is as vacuous as the preceding one. Does *anyone,* including Professor Walker, deny the proposition I have just set forth? Alternatively, is the distinguishing criterion a belief in one or both of the following propositions: that *only* leaders ought to be committed to democratic norms and that "widespread apathy and general political incompetence" are *desirable* features of representative democratic republics? If so, this criterion very seriously misrepresents, I believe, most of the writers he cites, and probably all of them.

(2) One central difficulty with Professor Walker's paradigm is, I think, that he insists upon interpreting as if they were normative or deontological certain writings that were mainly if not wholly intended to set out descriptive, empirical theories. Most (though perhaps not all) of the works cited by Professor Walker are not attempts to prescribe how democracy *ought* to work but to *describe* how some of the political systems widely called by that name do in fact operate and to *explain* why they operate this way. Professor Walker may deplore the neglect of normative questions, as many other political scientists and political philosophers do; but he ought not to confuse attempts at empirical description and explanation with efforts at prescribing how these systems ought to operate in order to attain desirable or ideal ends. I would not argue that every writer cited by Professor Walker has always tried to maintain this distinction or, if he did, has always succeeded; but I do think it is a serious misunderstanding to interpret these writers as essentially normative theorists.

At the empirical level, experience with and systematic study of political life in cities and countries with democratic governments has turned up evidence that, if valid, raises interesting and important empirical questions. To take the most obvious example, there is the enormous mass of evidence, much of it furnished by Professor Walker's colleagues in the Survey Research Center of the University of Michigan, on rates of participation in political life. This evidence seems to demonstrate, rather conclusively I think, that rates of participation vary widely, that a rather large fraction of adults participate in political life barely at all, and that a small proportion of adults participate a very great deal. Confronted by this evidence, political scientists have had either to reject it as factually false, which it is increasingly difficult to do; or to accept it provisionally as factually correct. If it is approximately correct, what do we make of it? As I see it, evidence of this kind confronts us with problems for both empirical and normative theory. Strictly at the level of empirical analysis and explanation we face such questions as: How do we account for these variations in rates of participation? How do these variations affect the outcome of elections, government policy-making, etc.? Even after we have arrived at necessarily tentative and provisional answers to these empirical questions, important normative questions, which I shall not try to formulate here, would still remain unanswered. The point seems too obvious to be worth stressing, but attempts to *explain* should not be confounded with attempts to *prescribe*.

One more example: there is substantial evidence on the distribution of American attitudes toward civil liberties and certain other norms associated with (though perhaps not inextricably bound up with) democratic behavior. As Professor Walker rightly says in a footnote, the evidence is not conclusive. Further research may prove it wrong; I, for one, hope that the present evidence for the existence of considerably less than a widespread and confident commitment to democratic and libertarian norms will be found wrong. Meanwhile, it is the best evidence we have, it cannot be brushed aside, and it cannot be rewritten to fit our hopes. If we accept the evidence, even provisionally, it suggests important problems both for empirical analysis and explanation and for normative analysis and prescription. Strictly at the empirical level, the evidence suggests a paradox: in a "democratic" country like the United States, where elections take place regularly, why aren't anti-libertarian and even anti-democratic norms transmuted into national policy more often than they are? How does it happen that on matters of free speech, for example, some norms that seem to be weakly held or even opposed by a majority of citizens are nonetheless applied vigorously by the Supreme Court, enforced by the executive branch, and at least tolerated by the Congress? The question, you will note, is formulated as an empirical one. Obviously the answer has a bearing on normative theory as well. But Professor Walker, so it appears to me, persists in interpreting an empirical enterprise ("I must try to understand and *explain* this curious phenomenon") as if it were explicitly or implicitly a normative enterprise of mounting a defense of the status quo ("I must try to *justify* this curious phenomenon").

I may, however, do Professor Walker an injustice, since I confess that his presentation leaves me uncertain as to exactly where he stands: that is, whether (a) he rejects the survey *evidence* on such matters as participation and the distribution of democratic norms; or (b) he accepts the evidence (contingently, which is all anyone can properly do with empirical data) but rejects the *explanations* of Key, Truman, and others; or (c) he accepts both the evidence and the explanation but denies that they describe (or prescribe) a desirable state of affairs in a democracy. If it is the first, which I doubt, we must await his own evidence. If it is the second—I so interpret his argument about apathy—we must await the development of his own theory and his testing of it; I return to this point later on. If it is the third, I heartily concur. I imagine that most of the other people he treats as "elitists" would also concur.

(3) Professor Walker's confounding of empirical explanation with prescription tempts him, I fear, to play the part of Procrustes and force his theorists to fit the bed he has prepared for them. The cut may be small—a half-inch slice off the top of a writer's head may seem important to no one but that author; or it may be rather large—from the ears up, say.

Exquisitely painful as they are to the victims, examples of the first sort are, it seems, so tedious in the telling that the suffering of the persistent reader finally surpasses that of the victims. I shall therefore spare the reader this unpleasantness. But may I offer one or two examples of surgery on a more ambitious scale?

Professor Walker describes the views of the "elitists" as follows: "The elitist theory allows the citizen only a passive role as an object of political activity; he exerts influence on policy making only by rendering judgments after-the-fact in national elections." It is unclear whether Professor Walker regards this as (1) an incorrect empirical statement; (2) a correct—or roughly correct—empirical statement; or (3) a description of what the authors he cites regard as a desirable state of affairs. I confess that I find it far too simple to be acceptable. And clearly an author who subscribed to this as a roughly accurate empirical statement—indeed, I have the impression that Professor Walker himself believes it to be correct—need not regard this state of affairs as the least bit desirable, unless, perhaps, in the weak sense that even worse states are possible. With the next sentence, Professor Walker renders his elitists more frankly normative: "The safety of contemporary democracy lies in the high-minded sense of responsibility of its leaders, the *only* elements of society who are *actively striving to discover and implement the common good*" (my italics). Strangely, at this point Professor Walker cites no writer who made such a statement; personally, I find the sentence equally preposterous as an empirical statement or as a prescription for a desirable state of affairs.

Finally, Professor Walker concludes his paragraph by hammering his point home with a quotation that, like many other readers, I read initially as a devastating confirmation of his interpretation of the "elitists." The sentence reads as follows: "The citizens are left to 'judge a world they never made, and thus to become a genteel counterpart of the mobs which sporadically unseated aristocratic governments in eighteenth- and nineteenth-century Europe.' " In heaven's name, I thought to myself, which of his "elitists" ever made such an astounding statement! The footnote led me to an article not by any of the writers he is attacking but by Lane Davis, who, like Professor Walker, evidently is also a critic of the so-called elitist theory. Thus we enter into the world of the closed circle of mutually reinforcing scholarship, where one critic of X cites a fellow critic of X in order to establish the validity of his own interpretation of X. Soon it will be quite unnecessary to examine what X said or seek to interpret X in the light of what can be understood about X's intentions. Walker will simply cite what Davis says X means, then Davis can cite Walker's article citing Davis' article interpreting X, then, . . . Poor X!

May I offer one more example of Professor Walker's somewhat uninhibited selection and interpretation? He writes: "It has also been suggested by several elitist theorists that democracies have good reason to fear increased political participation. They argue that a successful (that is, stable) democratic system depends on widespread apathy and general political imcompetence."

Who are the "several elitist theorists" who have made statements equivalent to those two sentences and particularly the second? We are directed to the whole of Chapter 14 in Berelson *et al.* I find it curious that Professor Walker was unable to cite anything more precise than the whole chapter. As readers of that chapter will recall, a central aspect of it is to contrast a hypothetical normative democratic theory prescribing certain kinds and levels of behavior with the findings on actual behavior in Elmira. The authors then seek to explain how, despite the gap, the system does function. Sometimes they also make normative comments. But I think the reader . . . will find that even their normative comments do not justify Professor Walker's statement.[9]

We are also directed to Lipset, but probably as a result of differing printings the pages cited take me to the Table of Contents of my own edition of *Political Man*—or else to two blank pages of the edition of Michels' *Political Parties* that Lipset edited. However, if Professor Walker had looked through Lipset's writings for a full and fair interpretation, as I am sure he did, he must surely have noticed some statements that do not support the cynical view of civic participation suggested by the sentence that Professor Walker has written.[10]

In sum, I have serious reservations as to the validity of Professor Walker's citations on this matter.[11] I fear, too, that he is led by his fixed ideas of "elitist theorists" into substituting, albeit unconsciously, extreme interpretations of his authors for their own much more balanced, qualified, and complex formulations. In terms of what I take to be his own aspirations for theory, this is a pity. Cutting down straw men is not going to answer the very hard questions nor overcome the very real deficiencies of democratic theory.

(4) The passage I have just been criticizing illustrates another aspect of Professor Walker's critique that I find particularly painful. Even if we were to assume that he correctly interprets "several" of the writers he calls "elitist," what of the others who hold very different views? If the writers happen to disagree among themselves, by what criterion does Professor Walker determine who is, and who is not, an elitist? Are we to take every item from someone's writings that lends itself to an "elitist" interpretation and neglect every item that does not?

Speaking for myself, I disagree strongly with the notion that high rates of political participation in democratic orders necessarily lead to, or must inevitably be associated with, "instability." I disagree even more strongly with the view that the rates of political participation that have been characteristic of the American citizen body—or, for that matter, the citizen body of any large national polyarchal system—are desirable. On the contrary, I happen to believe that they are deplorably low. I should like to see much higher rates of political activity, particularly among some segments of the population whose participation has been lowest. But there are worlds of difference among different factors that might lead to higher participation and worlds of difference in the quality and value of acts of participation. The rapid rise in electoral participation in the late years of the Weimar Republic did not make it a "better" democracy, nor did it enable that Republic to solve its problems. Instead, it was associated with factors that transformed that experiment in democracy into a monstrous system with very high rates of "participation" of a kind and where apathy was encouraged only in the concentration camps.[12]

This not a recent point of view on my part, nor, I imagine, is it one with which many of the writers cited by Professor

Walker would disagree. I would not expect Professor Walker to have read everything I have written, but I am flattered to think that he has read the books he cites. I should therefore like to remind him of some passages in these books.[13] One of the curious ironies of his method of selection is that while he interprets empirical theory as if it were normative or prescriptive, he seems to have overlooked some efforts to formulate normative criteria for the performance of democracies or polyarchies.[14] Thus in *A Preface to Democratic Theory,* working out some ideas Lindblom and I had already advanced in *Politics, Economics, and Welfare,* I tried to develop a set of standards against which it would (in theory) be possible to measure the performance of a political system in order to determine the degree to which that system "maximized democracy." The eight standards I laid down were, I thought, extremely severe. In fact, I wrote: "I think it may be laid down dogmatically that no human organization —certainly none with more than a handful of people—has ever met or is ever likely to meet these eight conditions." [15] I defined "polyarchies," however, as political systems in which the eight conditions "exist to a relatively high degree" (p. 84). I advanced the proposition that "polyarchy is a function of the political activity of the members" (p. 81) but also conjectured that "if an increase in political activity brings the authoritarian-minded into the political arena, consensus on the basic norms among the politically active certainly must be declining. To the extent that consensus declines, we would expect . . . that, after some lag, polyarchy would also decline" (p. 89).

Professor Walker may not agree with any of this. But I do not understand why he ignores it in order to construct his paradigm of "elitist theory."

In short, I do not share Professor Walker's confidence that he knows the implicit or explicit normative assumptions of the writers he has tried to summarize. Whether they would agree, in the main, on their empirical descriptions is one thing; whether they would agree, in the main, on their normative standards and conclusions is quite another. My guess is that although they would not agree with Professor Walker's description of them in either case, their actual normative disagreements would prove more profound than their empirical disagreements. But I do not pretend to know.

II

One possible justification for building a man of straw in order to attack it is the methodological (and psychological?) assistance even a straw man may give in designing one's own alternative theory. I cannot help feeling that Professor Walker's caricature is intended for this purpose: it provides him with at least a hypothetical view to react against. Perhaps we should take it in that spirit.

In any case, when Professor Walker turns his attention from his *bêtes noires* in order to speculate about apathy and social movements, he says much with which it is difficult to disagree. Thus when he speaks of "widespread political apathy... among many sectors of the American public," who will contest his statement that "it is important to ask why this is so and not simply to explain how this phenomenon contributes to the smooth functioning of the system"?

In fact, it seems to me that in the last two decades there has been more attention paid to the extent, types, characteristics, and possible causes of varying rates of political participation than in the preceding 25 centuries. Perhaps the best evidence on this point is supplied by Professor Walker himself. Not only does he rely heavily in his own theoretical suggestions on the work of social scientists who, by the standards of the first part of his essay, would surely be classified as elitists," but his hypotheses, as I read them, do not go much beyond what is already in the mainstream of the social sciences.[16]

Nonetheless, Professor Walker is surely right that we do not know nearly as much as we ought to, that political apathy, alienation, indifference, lack of confidence, and feelings of inefficacy are widespread in the United States among the poor, Negroes, and even many individuals and segments in other strata, and that these feelings create obstacles to effective participation in political life. I assume that Professor Walker and I are at one in wanting these obstacles to be eliminated and in thinking that political scientists may have something to contribute to this task.

If much of what Professor Walker has to say about apathy and participation is, as I believe, pretty much taken for granted by most students of the subject, he has nonetheless contributed some interesting additional hypotheses that have not, so far as I know, been studied. I have in mind, for example, his intriguing speculation that "high crime (or suicide) rates and low rates of voting may very well be related." It is a pity that Professor Walker did not go beyond speculation in order to furnish us with some tests of his hypothesis. To be sure, the problem has formidable aspects, but even a brief survey of the evidence would have been helpful.[17]

Professor Walker's references to the possible effects of the American political system on participation and apathy call attention to a methodological matter that until recently has generally been ignored: the need to examine the problem in a comparative framework and not exclusively in the American setting. The evidence of a few comparative studies suggests a paradox.[18] Although turnout in elections is relatively low in the United States, political involvement, interest, and participation in politics in ways other than voting is relatively high: quite possibly higher than in any other large country. Apathy, alienation, and nonparticipation are not peculiar to the United States; indeed, a good case could be made out that these phenomena are present to a lesser degree in the United States than in most other democracies. It would be premature to fix on this conclusion. My point is that to understand the problems Professor Walker is concerned with we need more analysis across nations as well as within the United States itself.

III

Professor Walker's suggestions for further study of "social movements" is timely. If we adopt Professor Heberle's definition of a social movement as "a stirring among the people, an unrest, a collective attempt to reach a visualized goal, especially a change in certain social institutions,"[19] surely it is true that parties, pressure groups, interest groups, voting behavior, and many other closely related topics have been far more popular than social movements as subjects of investigation by American political scientists. But I wonder if the reasons for this relative neglect are really where Professor Walker locates them. Well-defined social movements—the anti-slavery movement of the pre-Civil War period or the agrarian discontent of the 1880's and 1890's—are comparatively rare in the United States. It is no accident that it is mainly historians who have written about American social movements, for the examples are chiefly historical. Social movements are often short-lived, as in the case of the Know-nothings before the Civil War. If they endure, they inevitably become institutionalized; when they do become institutionalized, as in the case of the Prohibition movement, the labor movement, or the Socialist Party, they are more likely to be studied by political scientists, under more familiar rubrics, e.g., pressure groups, interest groups, or political parties.[20]

To the extent that social movements have been amorphous and fugitive they have left little permanent evidence to study. Moreover, an older bias in favor of research in the library rather than in the field would probably handicap political scientists. My impression is that today, when political scientists get out into the field more rapidly than once might have been the case, they are more likely to observe social movements in the earlier stages. Thus the Radical Right, whose adherents are not always easy to examine, has nonetheless been the subject of a good deal of recent inquiry.[21]

It is too early to tell whether the civil rights movement, the recent peace and anti-Vietnam-war movements, the New Left, and student discontent will receive much professional attention from political scientists. I venture to guess that the amount of attention paid to them by political scientists will depend in very large measure on how long they last.

In any case, Professor Walker is surely right in suggesting that movements like these are important to study. I would only add two cautionary notes. First, as with political participation, the subject cries out for treatment in a comparative and historical framework.[22] Second, considering the variety of phenomena that might be called social movements and the great variety in the "relationship of challenge and response between the established political system and social movements," to use Professor Walker's phrase, the subject would be unmanageable, I fear, with a framework no more specific than Professor Walker provides us in his essay. Some typologies, some specific hypotheses would, I imagine, go a long way toward making the subject more manageable. Efforts in this direction might be a good deal more productive than a general exhortation to go out and study social movements.

IV

There is a danger that the main thrust of Professor Walker's essay will seem to have been lost in all these details. Insofar as his essay is an appeal for better normative democratic theory than now seems to be at hand, I most enthusiastically concur.

Even if there is a renascence of normative theory, as Professor Walker and I hope there will be, I doubt very much whether there will ever be an entity that we can call *the* normative theory of democracy. Despite the frequency and confidence with which the "classic theory of democracy" is often described, there has never been such a theory. Between Aristotle and Paine, as between Rousseau and Mill, there are universes of difference. Along with other people, theorists who believe in popular government have never agreed wholly on the goals or values to be maximized. Equally important, they have never agreed on the kinds and degrees of constraints that have to be treated as fixed by the conditions of man and society, whether for all time or within a given period. Disagreement with respect to these basic assumptions is not going to disappear. We should therefore expect that in the future as in the past there will be not one but a number of differing normative theories of democracy. But I agree with Professor Walker: it is time to get on with the job.

NOTES

1. See, for example, his comment: "It is popular leaders who, by referring all issues to the decision of the people, are responsible for substituting the sovereignty of decrees for that of laws." See also his comments on "the particular causes of revolution and change" in democracies, e.g., "In democracies changes are chiefly due to the wanton license of demogogues." *The Politics of Aristotle,* trans. with an introduction, notes, and appendixes by Ernest Barker (Oxford University Press, 1952), pp. 168, 215.

2. In the *Discourses,* after noting that two "principi virtuosi" in succession were sufficient to conquer the world—Philip of Macedon and Alexander the Great—Machiavelli goes on to say: "Il che tanto più debba fare una republica, avendo per il modo dello eleggere non solamente due successioni ma infiniti principi virtuoissimi che sono l'uno dell'altro successori: la quale virtuosa successioné fia sempre in ogni republica bene ordinata." *Libro Primo Dei Discorsi Sopra Le Prima Deca di Tito Livio,* XX, in *Tutte Le Opere Storiche E Letterarie di Niccolò Machiavelli,* Mazzoni and Casella (eds.), (Florence, B. Barbéra, 1929), p. 90.

3. He lamented, for example, that men of true merit (*virtù*) are sought for in difficult times but in easy times it is not virtuous men who are most favored but those with riches and the proper relations; in peaceful times, other citizens who are jealous of the reputation of the virtuous want not merely to be their equals but their superiors. Book 3, XVI, *ibid.,* p. 224. See also *ibid.* XXVIII, pp. 239 ff.

4. *Du Contrat Social,* Chap. IV. "De la démocratie," pp. 280–281. Note his comment: "Il est contre l'ordre naturel que le grand nombre gouverne et que let petit soit gouverné" (Paris, Éditions Garnier Frères, 1962), p. 280.

5. *Ibid.,* p. 282.

6. *On Liberty and Considerations on Representative Government,* ed. by R. B. McCallum (New York, Macmillan, 1947), pp. 215–216.

7. May I register a dissent seemingly so minor that I fear it will appear to be nitpicking: the appropriateness of the label? I realize that Professor Walker has taken the expression "the elitist theory of

democracy" from Lipset; but even if Lipset may have had his reasons while writing a preface to the major work of Michels for applying this phrase to Weber, Schumpeter, Parsons, and James Burnham, that is not a good reason for stretching it, as Professor Walker does, to cover others. I, for one, object to being labelled "elitist" not only because—as I hope to show—it would be inaccurate in implication even if it were a neutral term, but even more so because in our language and in our society it is unavoidably, I think, a pejorative, even a polemical epithet.

To substitute epithet for argument was, I am sure, not Professor Walker's intention. Nonetheless, to stick the label "elitist" on someone is to discredit half his argument without saying another word. Moreover, precisely because the term "elite" carries many of the connotations that Professor Walker and most others are inclined to read into it—no matter how much an author may try to sterilize the term by definition—I have generally avoided the term in writing about American politics. Like David Truman and V. O. Key, I have used terms rather more descriptive and discriminating, so it seems to me, such as political leadership, political strata, and the like. It is revealing, incidentally, that in the index to V. O. Key's *Public Opinion and American Democracy* the only reference to "elite" reads as follows: "elite: *see* political activists." I suggest that this difference in the choice of words is more than a mere matter of taste or distaste for certain labels. It also reflects a conviction on the part of Key, Truman, myself, and others that "elitist" interpretations of American political life are inadequate both empirically and normatively. The extent to which Professor Walker has misunderstood the orientation of the late V. O. Key, Jr., is best indicated by the work that Key was writing at the time of his death, and that Professor Walker could not have read, of course, when he wrote his article. "The perverse and unorthodox argument of this little book," Key wrote, "is that voters are not fools. To be sure, many individual voters act in odd ways indeed; yet in the large the electorate behaves about as rationally and responsibly as we should expect, given the clarity of the alternatives presented to it and the character of information available to it." *The Responsible Electorate* (Cambridge: Harvard University Press, 1966), p. 7.

8. Why, by the way, not also: Campbell, Converse, Miller, Stokes, Downs, Sartori, Almond, Verba, Kornhauser, Lasswell, Lane, Tingsten . . . ? In short: among writers who have examined questions of leadership and participation, who is *not* eligible for Professor Walker's list?

9. Here are some of them, with italics added to emphasize the difference between what they say and what Professor Walker says they say: "The democratic citizen is expected to be well informed about political affairs. . . . By such standards the voter falls short. Even when he has the motivation, he finds it difficult to make decisions on the basis of full information when the subject is relatively simple and proximate; how can he do so when it is complex and remote? . . .": *Voting* (Chicago: University of Chicago Press, 1954), p. 308. "How could a mass democracy work if *all* the people were deeply involved in politics? Lack of interest by *some* people is not without its benefits, too. . . . Extreme interest goes with extreme

partisanship and *might* culminate in rigid fanaticism that *could* destroy democratic processes *if* generalized throughout the community. . . . *Some* people are and should be highly interested in politics, but not *everyone* is or needs to be. Only the doctrinaire would depreciate the *moderate indifference* that facilitates compromise ": *ibid.*, pp. 314–315; "*The classical political philosophers were right in the direction of their assessment of the virtues of the citizen. But they demanded those virtues in too extreme or doctrinal a form. The voter does have some principles, he does have information and rationality, he does have interest—but he does not have them in the extreme, elaborate, comprehensive, or detailed form* in which they were uniformly recommended by political philosophers": *ibid.*, p. 322.

10. Like many other writers on politics, including Rousseau, Lipset's writings contain statements which, quoted out of context, might seem to offer faint confirmation for the interpretation offered by Professor Walker. But I do not see how, for example, Lipset's chapter on "Elections: Who Votes and Who Doesn't?" in *Political Man* could be regarded by anyone who reads the whole chapter as yielding the sentence in Professor Walker's essay; see especially pp. 181, 186.

11. The third citation is to an article by Morris-Jones, which I do not have at hand as I write. If it turns out that he has correctly interpreted Morris-Jones, would that justify his interpretation of Berelson *et al.* and of Lipset?

12. Incidentally, while we may have recently emphasized the conditions of democratic "stability" too much, and the conditions of democratic change too little, I doubt whether anyone who remembers the failure of "stable" democracies to emerge in the USSR, Italy, Germany, and Spain will ever find it in himself to scoff at writers who focus on the conditions of democratic stability. What such writers are likely to have in mind when they think of democratic "instability" is not cabinet changes nor even piddling differences in regime but the possibility of democratic failures eventuating in brutal dictatorships in comparison with which even the worst polyarchy will seem like the promised land.

13. In *Politics, Economics, and Welfare,* Lindblom and I wrote: "Polyarchy also requires a relatively high degree of political activity. That is, enough people must participate in the governmental process so that political leaders compete for the support of a large and more or less representative cross section of the population. . . .

"Admittedly this is a rather imprecise formulation; in what follows we shall attempt to refine it a little. But one cannot be very precise. . . . In practice, moreover, even in one country the extent of political activity varies enormously from one policy-making situation to another, from complete apathy to widespread activity. Then, too, political "activity" is itself a difficult kind of behavior to measure. The number of variables is large, including the number of people involved, the intensity with which they pursue their goals, the type of activity they indulge in, the political position and location of those who are active, their status, degree of control over others, and so on. . . .

" . . . In a very large number of important governmental decisions only a small minority of the electorate expresses or apparently even possesses any definite preferences at all among the alternatives in dispute. And it is equally safe to say that very little specific national policy is ever a product of an expressed preference for a specific by an overwhelming majority of the electorate. . . .

". . . In practice, then, the democratic goal that governmental decisions should accord with the preferences of the greater number of adults in the society is extraordinarily difficult to approximate, and rarely, if ever, is it closely approximated. . . .

". . . This discrepancy between polyarchy and democracy arouses anxieties among those who wish to approximate democracy more closely, and rightly so. Keeping this fact in mind, let us suggest some general lines of approach to the question of the level of political activity required as a precondition for polyarchy.

"A considerable measure of political inactivity is not *by itself* a sign that the democratic goal is not being roughly approximated by a polyarchy. . . .

". . . The question, then, is not so much whether citizens are active but whether they have the opportunity to exert control through activity when they wish to do so. . . .

". . . Therefore the problem is not so much one of insuring that every citizen is politically active on every issue as it is one of insuring that all citizens have approximately equal opportunity to act, using 'opportunity' in a realistic rather than legalistic sense. . . .

". . . Equal opportunity to act is not, however, a product merely of legal rights. It is a product of a variety of factors that make for differences in understanding the key points in the political process, access to them, methods of exploiting this access, optimism and buoyancy about the prospect of success, and willingness to act. Some of these factors probably cannot be rationally influenced given the present state of knowledge and techniques. Three that to some extent can are income, wealth, and education. A fourth that may become important as knowledge increases is personality. . . .

". . . Nevertheless, many policy decisions cannot actually reflect any specific preferences of the greater number. About the most that can be said for polyarchy is that, if the opportunities for political action are kept open to a representative section of the adult population, specific policies will rarely violate highly ranked, intense, stable, and relatively broad preferences of the greater number for a longer period than about the interval between elections. . . ." (pp. 309–314).

14. Thus in *Politics, Economics and Welfare,* Lindblom and I offered "Seven Basic Ends for Social Action": freedom, rationality, democracy, subjective equality, security, progress, and appropriate inclusion. Of democracy we wrote as follows:

"The democratic goal is twofold. It consists of a condition to be attained and a principle guiding the procedure for attaining it. The condition is political equality, which we define as follows: *Control over governmental decisions is shared so that the preferences of no one citizen are weighted more heavily than the preferences of any other one citizen.* The principle is majority rule, which we define as follows: *Governmental decisions should be controlled by the greater number expressing their preferences in the 'last say.'*

"Democracy is a goal, not an achievement. The main sociopolitical process for approximating (although not achieving) democracy we shall call polyarchy. The characteristics of polyarchy, its prerequisites, and its significance as a device for rational social action on economic matters are discussed in a later chapter. If democracy is one of our goals and if polyarchy is a process for approximating that goal, it follows that we must also value polyarchy as a means. But here we are concerned with the democratic goal itself" (p. 41).

15. (p. 71.) Though I have always tried to write lucidly, I am increasingly appalled by incontrovertible evidence of my inability to do so. If Professor Walker interprets as normative theory what I (and, as I believe, others) wholly or primarily intended to be empirical theory, others have reversed the process by interpreting my ventures in normative theorizing as if I were describing the American political system. Despite the clear warning contained in the sentence just cited, the fact that my model of "polyarchy" and my description of "The American Hybrid" are in the same book, though in separate chapters, is evidently enough to lead to their being confounded. Cf. Robert E. Agger, Daniel Goldrich, and Bert E. Swanson, *The Rulers and the Ruled* (Wiley, New York, 1964), pp. 93 ff. Incidentally, my guess, supported by some data, is that if a number of "democracies" were measured by the standards of polyarchal performance described in the model, the United States would be found to rank well down the list. A highly innovative attempt to undertake such a ranking is Deane Neubauer's "On the Theory of Polyarchy: An Empirical Study of Democracy in Ten Countries" (unpublished doctoral dissertation, Yale University, 1965).

16. Many of the factors Professor Walker advances as possible explanations for varying degrees of political involvement-apathy, or political participation-nonparticipation, will be found in the pioneering article, published in 1954, by Lipset, Lazarsfeld, Barton, and Linz, "The Psychology of Voting: An Analysis of Political Behavior," *Handbook of Social Psychology* (Cambridge, Mass., Addison-Wesley, 1954), Vol. II, pp. 1124–1175. A decade later, Angus Campbell presented a compact, succinct, and (to me) potentially powerful explanatory theory that takes into account much of the work in the interval: "The Passive Citizen" in Stein Rokkan, ed., *Approaches to the Study of Political Participation* (Bergen, The Chr. Michelsen Institute, 1962).

17. Although reported crime rates are, for a variety of reasons, notoriously unreliable indices of actual crime, investigation conceivably might turn up some connections. However, as to the relation between suicide rates and voting rates, an examination made at my request by Edward R. Tufte of readily available evidence shows that in the United States the relationship, if any, runs counter to Professor Walker's conjecture. Taking each state as a unit, there is a positive and not a negative relationship between suicides and voting turnout. The correlations are 0.24 with turnout in Presidential elections and 0.34 with turnout in off-year elections for governor and Senators. Mississippi has the lowest turnout and the second lowest suicide rate. Rhode Island, which has the lowest suicide rate, has a high voting turnout, while Wyoming, which has about the same turnout as Rhode Island, has the second highest suicide

rate. California and New York had almost exactly the same turnout in the 1960 Presidential election, but the suicide rate in California is 16 per 100,000, putting it in the highest group, while New York at 9.7 per 100,000 is among the lowest. Professor Walker's hypothesis would imply that the suicide rate among Negroes is higher than among whites; in fact, for the United States the rate among whites (11.4) is more than twice that among Negroes (4.5). In fact the rate among nonwhites is lower than among whites in all states except six with few nonwhites. In eleven Southern states the correlation between suicide rates and voting in Presidential elections (which according to the conjecture should of course be negative) is positive and moderately high: 0.47; with off-term elections for governor and Senators, it is lower but still positive: 0.36. The correlation of suicide rates with voting in off-term elections for governor and Senators is practically identical in North and South; with voting in Presidential elections, the correlation in the North is almost nonexistent but negative: 0.17. The data are from Louis I. Dublin, *Suicide* (New York, Ronald Press, 1963), pp. 218–219, and Herbert Jacob and Kenneth Vines (eds.), *Politics in the American States* (Boston: Little, Brown, 1965), pp. 40, 46. My strong impression is that if the hypothesis were checked against comparative data, it would run into similar difficulties. For example, the Scandinavian countries have similar voting rates; yet while the suicide rate is high in Sweden and Denmark, it is low in Norway. Italy, which has astonishingly high turnout, has a low suicide rate, etc.

18. I have in mind particularly Gabriel Almond and Sidney Verba, *The Civic Culture* (Princeton: Princeton University Press, 1963); and Philip E. Converse and Georges Dupeux, "Politicization of the Electorate in France and the United States," *Public Opinion Quarterly,* 26 (Spring, 1962), 11–113; and Rokkan (ed.), *Approaches to the Study of Political Participation, op. cit.*

19. Rudolf Heberle, *Social Movements* (New York, Appleton-Century-Crofts, 1951), p. 6.

20. Professor Walker may have been somewhat misled because he has looked for studies of "social movements" under the wrong headings. Standard texts on political parties and pressure groups have for decades contained descriptions of farmers' organizations, the labor movement, the NAACP, etc., under such headings as "pressure groups" or "interest groups." They have also treated third parties, sometimes extensively. E.g., the third edition of V. O. Key's *Politics, Parties, and Pressure Groups* (New York, Thomas Y. Crowell Co., 1952), which had chapters in Part I, Pressure Groups, on "Agrarianism" that included a section on "Cycles of Agrarian Discontent: The Nature of Political Movements"; "Workers," "Business," and "Other Interest Groups," including "Racial and Nationalist Minorities." See also Chapter 7, "The Party Battle, 1896–1952" and Chapter 11, "The Role of Minor Parties."

21. The best known work is, of course, *The New American Right,* Daniel Bell (ed.) (New York: Criterion Books, 1955), and the "expanded and updated" version *The Radical Right* (New York: Doubleday, 1963). In 1963, *The Journal of Social Issues* devoted an entire issue to "American Political Extremism in the 1960's" (Vol. 19, April, 1963). And see the results of a direct attempt to interview

people at a San Francisco Regional School of Anti-Communism by
R. E. Wolfinger, B. K. Wolfinger, K. Prewitt and S. Rosenhack,
"America's Radical Right: Politics and Ideology," in *Ideology and
Discontent,* David Apter (ed.) (New York: The Free Press of
Glencoe, 1964).

22. Comparable, for example, to Otto Kirchheimer's "Confining Condi-
tions and Revolutionary Breakthroughs," *American Political Science
Review,* 59 (December, 1965), 964–974; or Val R. Lorwin's "Labor
Organizations and Politics in Belgium and France," in *National
Labor Movements in the Postwar World,* E. M. Kassalow (ed.)
(Evanston: Northwestern University Press, 1963), pp. 142–168; and
his "Reflections on the History of the French and American Labor
Movements," *Journal of Economic History* (March, 1957), 24–244.

6: The Case for Decentralization

PAUL GOODMAN

Throughout society, the centralizing style of organization has been pushed so far as to become ineffectual, economically wasteful, humanly stultifying, and ruinous to democracy. There are overcentralized systems in industry, in government, in culture, and in agriculture. The tight interlocking of these systems has created a situation in which modest, direct, and independent action has become extremely difficult in every field. The only remedy is a strong admixture of decentralism. The problem is where, how much, and how to go about it.

Let me give some rough definitions. In a centralized enterprise, the function to be performed is the goal of the organization rather than of persons (except as they identify with the organization). The persons are personnel. Authority is top-

From *People or Personnel* (New York: Random House, Inc., 1963), pp. 3–27. Copyright © 1963, 1964, and 1965 by Paul Goodman. Reprinted by permission of the author and publisher.

down. Information is gathered from below in the field and is processed to be usable by those above; decisions are made in headquarters; and policy, schedule, and standard procedure are transmitted downward by chain of command. The enterprise as a whole is divided into departments of operation to which are assigned personnel with distinct roles, to give standard performance. This is the system in Mr. Goldwater's department store, in the Federal government and in the State governments, in General Motors and in the UAW, in the New York public schools and in many universities, in most hospitals, in neighborhood renewal, in network broadcasting and the Associated Press, and in the deals that chain-grocers make with farmers. The system was devised to discipline armies; to keep records, collect taxes, and perform bureaucratic functions; and for certain kinds of mass production. It has now become pervasive.

The principle of decentralism is that people are engaged in a function and the organization is how they cooperate. Authority is delegated away from the top as much as possible and there are many accommodating centers of policy-making and decision. Information is conveyed and discussed in face-to-face contacts between field and headquarters. Each person becomes increasingly aware of the whole operation and works at it in his own way according to his capacities. Groups arrange their own schedules. Historically, this system of voluntary association has yielded most of the values of civilization, but it is thought to be entirely unworkable under modern conditions and the very sound of it is strange.

I

Now if, lecturing at a college, I happen to mention that some function of society which is highly centralized could be much decentralized without loss of efficiency, or perhaps with a gain in efficiency, at once the students want to talk about nothing else. This insistence of theirs used to surprise me, and I tested it experimentally by slipping in a decentralist remark during lectures on entirely different subjects. The students unerringly latched on to the remark. In their questions, for twenty minutes they might pursue the main theme—e.g., nuclear pacifism or even the sexual revolution—but they returned to decentralization for many hours, attacking me with skepticism, hot objections, or hard puzzlers.

From their tone, it is clear that in this subject something is at stake for their existence. They feel trapped in the present system of society that allows them so little say or initiative, and that indeed is like the schooling that they have been enduring for twelve to sixteen years. The querulousness and biting sarcasm mean that, if decentralization *is* possible, they have become needlessly resigned; they hotly defend the second best that they have opted for instead. But the serious and hard questions are asked with a tone of skeptical wistfulness that *I* will be able to resolve all difficulties. If I confess at some point that I don't know the answer, at once students invent answers for me, to prove that decentralization *is* possible after all.

Naturally, at each college we go over much the same ground. The very sameness of the discussions is disheartening evidence that the centralist style exists as a mass-superstition, never before questioned in the students' minds. If I point to some commonplace defect of any centralized system, or one which leaps to the eye in the organization of their own college, I am regarded as a daring sage. No other method of organization was conceived as possible. . . .

II

Decentralization is not lack of order or planning, but a kind of coordination that relies on different motives from top-down direction, standard rules, and extrinsic rewards like salary and status to provide integration and cohesiveness. It is not "anarchy." (But of course, most Anarchists, like the anarcho-syndicalists or the community-anarchists, have not been "anarchists" either, but decentralists.)

As an example of decentralist coordination, the Anarchist Prince Kropotkin, who was a geographer, used to point spectacularly to the history of Western science from the heroic age of Vesalius, Copernicus, and Galileo to his own time of Pasteur, Kelvin, and J. J. Thomson. The progress of science in all fields was exquisitely coordinated. There were voluntary associations, publications, regional and international conferences. The Ph.D. system was devised to disseminate new research to several hundred university libraries. There was continual private correspondence, even across warring boundaries. Yet in this vast common enterprise, so amazingly productive, there was no central direction whatever.

The chief bond of cohesion was, of course, that all scientists had the common aim of exploring Nature, as well as their personal idiosyncrasies and their personal and clique rivalries. The delicate integration of effort occurred because they followed the new data or worked with the frontier theories. It was almost uniquely rare, so far as we know (the case of Mendel is famous), that important work dropped out of the dialogue.

In the past forty years, the organization of science has begun to rely heavily on central Institutes and Foundations, to choose areas of research, to select personnel, to grant funds. National governments have become the chief sponsors and, in a sense, directors of research. It is possible that, on balance, this mode of organization might produce better results. It is efficient in that there are, literally, more "scientists" and there is a proliferation of research products. Without doubt some methods, like population surveys, and some apparatus, like atom smashers and moon rockets, require a lot of capital and central organization. It has been argued that when knowledge accumulates beyond a certain point, its dissemination must be centrally directed and further research must be systematically directed.

Yet it is not self-evident that this style is superior to the private industriousness, lonely thought, shoestring apparatus of Pasteur, Edison, and Einstein or the master-disciple relations of Thomson, Rutherford, etc. Proof is difficult either way, for if the best brains are working in one style we cannot tell what they would be doing if working in another style. Even in technology and in the modern, centralized climate, as Ben Seligman has pointed out, "Since 1900, about half of the important inventions affecting consumer goods have come from independent researchers. Air-conditioning, automatic transmissions, cellophane, jet engines, and quick-freeze came from old-fashioned inventors or small companies."

The ideal test would be to try out both styles, but in fact the big central style eventually drives out the other, by non-scientific pressures. It buys up persons, dictates to the universities by grants for research and development, piles administrative and consultant duties on keen minds that would otherwise be working in philosophical seclusion or in real teaching. Some of the disadvantages are obvious. With the best will in the world, when so much capital and organization are invested there is a tendency toward immediate profits and military power, and there appears—astoundingly, in the history of Western science—commercial and political secrecy as a condition of research. Under authoritative direction, and with extrinsic rewards, a vast amount of "research" has been mere busywork. The pursuit of the goals of the organization, in "crash" programs, whether in medicine, strategy, or space exploration, necessarily has a different principle of order than the wandering dialogue of intellect with the unknown nature of things.

III

Over the centuries, not only scientific truth but most other objective values, like beauty or compassion, have thrived by voluntary association and independent solitude. (Theological salvation is perhaps the only spiritual good that has usually been centrally regulated.) Almost by definition, the progress of social justice has been by voluntary association, since the central authority is what is rebelled against. And, of course, to preserve liberty, the American political system was deliberately designed as a polarity of centralist and decentralist elements, with limitations on the power of the Sovereign and in-built checks and balances at every level.

But we must also remember that in its heyday, celebrated by Adam Smith, the free-enterprise system of partnerships and vigilant joint stockholders was in theory a model of decentralist coordination, as opposed to the centralized system of mercantilism, royal patents, and monopolies that it replaced. It reposed an absolute reliance on self-interest, voluntary association, and the cohesive influence of natural forces: Economic Man and the Laws of the Market. Pretty soon, however, the stockholders stopped attending to business and became absentee investors or even gamblers on the stock exchange. And almost from the beginning in this country, notably in the bank and the tariff, there was a revival of state monopolies.

IV

"How can you decentralize air-traffic control?" asks a student.

You can't. There are many functions that are central by their natures, and it is useful to enumerate some of the chief kinds.

Central authority is necessary where there are no district limits and something positive must be done, as in epidemic control or smog control; or when an arbitrary decision is required and there is no time for reflection, as in traffic control; or when we have to set arbitrary standards for a whole field, but the particular standard is indifferent, e.g., weights and measures or money.

Centralization is temporarily necessary when an emergency requires the concentration of all powers in a concerted effort. But history has shown that such emergency centralization can be fateful, for the central organization tends to outlive the emergency, and then its very existence creates a chronic emergency; people soon become helpless unless they are told what to do.

Central authority is convenient to perform routine or "merely" administrative functions, when people have more important things to do. This is the Marxist theory of the withering away of the State of "mere" administration. But this too can be fateful, for administration soon encroaches on every function. It is thus that the executive secretary of an organization ends up running the show.

Central organization is the most rational kind when the logistics of a situation outweigh consideration of the concrete particulars involved. These are all the cases of ticketing and tax collecting, where one person is like another. (E.g., a train ticket is technically a contract, but it would be absurd to negotiate each ticket individually.) In my opinion, the same holds for the mass production and distribution of any standard item that is good enough and that everybody needs.

Besides, there are monopolies that must be regulated and licensed by central authority (or nationalized), since by definition they cannot be countervailed. Some monopolies are natural or become so by circumstances, like urban water supply. Some enterprises become monopolistic because they are so heavily capitalized that competition is prohibitively risky or wasteful. They grow until they become the inevitable nature of things, and then must be so regulated. For instance, the railroads of Europe were decentrally planned and constructed, with voluntary agreement on gauges and schedules; but eventually, as monopolies, they have been nationalized and partly internationalized.

My bias is decentralist, yet in some functions I think we need more centralization than we have. For instance, there ought to be uniform modular standards in building materials and fixture. Building is a typical example of how we do things backwards. Where there ought to be decentralization, for instance in the design which requires artistry and in the decision of each neighborhood on how it wants to live, we get bureaucratic routine design, national policy, the standards of absentee sociologists, and the profits of promoters. But where there could be important savings, in materials and the process of construction, we do not standardize. Similarly, there ought to be standardization of machine parts and design, especially for domestic machinery and cars, to make repairs easier. And it is certainly absurd for the expensive enterprise of space exploration to be internationally competitive, instead of centrally planned and departmentalized with crews and honors shared.

Finally, automatic and computer technology is by nature highly centralizing, in its style and in its applications. This is a massive phenomenon of the present and immediate future and we shall recur to it continually. In general, the point of view of this book is that, where it is relevant, this technology should be maximized as quickly as possible and many such plants should be regulated as monopolies. But perhaps the profoundest problem that faces modern society is to decide *in what functions the automatic and computer style is not relevant, and there to curtail it or forget it.*

Thus, it is reasonable to use business machines in a branch-library system to expedite finding and exchanging books among the branches. But in my opinion, it is more dubious to select the books centrally and by computer, according to standards of excellence, consensus of the national reviews, etc.; for selection is a chief means of education and avenue of self-expression for each branch-librarian, and local attention is indispensable for the specific cultivation of each neighborhood. And in the children's section, even routine checking in and out provides unembarrassed occasions for conversation between the librarian and the children.

V

A Marxist student objects that blurring the division of labor, local option, face-to-face communication, and other decentralist positions are relics of a peasant ideology, provincial and illiberal.

There is something in this. In fact, there have always been two strands to decentralist thinking. Some authors, e.g., Laotse or Tolstoy, make a conservative peasant critique of centralized court and town as inorganic, verbal, and ritualistic. But other authors, e.g., Proudhon or Kropotkin, make a democratic urban critique of centralized bureaucracy and power, including feudal industrial power, as exploiting, inefficient, and discouraging to initiative. In our present era of State socialism, corporate feudalism, regimented schooling, brainwashing mass communications, and urban anomie, both kinds of critique make sense. We need to revive both peasant self-reliance and the democratic power of professional and technical guilds and workers' councils.

Any decentralization that could occur at present would inevitably be post-urban and post-centralist; it could not be provincial. There is no American who has not been formed by national TV and no region that has not been homogenized by the roads and chain stores. A model of twentieth-century decentralization is the Israeli *kibbutz*. Some would say that these voluntary communities are fanatical, but no one would deny that they are cosmopolitan and rationalistic, post-centralist and post-urban.

Decentralizing has its risks. Suppose that the school system of a Northern city were radically decentralized, given over to the control of the parents and teachers of each school. Without doubt some of the schools would be Birchite and some would be badly neglected. Yet it is hard to imagine that many schools could be worse than the present least-common-denominator. There would certainly be more experimentation. There would be meaningful other choices to move to. And inevitably all the schools would exist in a framework of general standards that they would have to measure up to or suffer the consequences.

Invariably, some student argues that without the intervention of the Federal government, the Negroes in the South will not get their civil rights. This may or may not be so, but certainly most of their progress toward civil rights so far has come from local action that has embarrassed and put pressure on Washington. By the same token the Negro organizations themselves have been decentrally coordinated; as Dr. King has pointed out, the "leadership" is continually following the localities. But the basic error of this student is to think that the "States' Rights" of the segregationists is decentralist. (As authentic regionalism *would* be decentralist.) If each locality indeed had its option, the counties where Negroes are in the majority would have very different rules! And they would provide a meaningful choice for other Negroes to move to.

VI

The relation of decentralization to physical and social mobility is an important topic; let us stay with it for another page. As the example of science has shown, it is possible to have decentralist community without territorial community. Yet decentralist philosophies have prized stability, "rootedness," subtle awareness of the environment, as a means to the integration of the domestic, technical, economic, political, and cultural functions of life and to provide a physical community in which the young can grow up.

The Americans have always been quick to form voluntary associations—Tocqueville mentions the trait with admiration; yet Americans have always been mobile—usually going *away,* individual and families leaving communities that did not offer opportunity, in order to try new territory known by hearsay. Historically, the country was open at the margins, because of either the geographical frontier or new jobs that attracted immigrants. When people settled, they again formed voluntary associations. Thus, to a degree, voluntary mobility favored decentralization. On the other hand, the new ties and settlements inevitably tended to become more homogeneous and national, the result of any uprooting.

At present, however, the country is closed at the margins, yet the physical (and social) mobility is even greater. Negroes migrate north because the sharecropping has failed and they are barred from the factories; Northern middle-class whites move to the suburbs to escape the Negroes; farm families have dwindled to 8 per cent. Unfortunately, none of these groups is moving *to* anything. And much moving is ordered by the central organization itself: national corporations send their employees and families to this or that branch; universities raid one another for staff; promoters and bureaucrats dislocate tenants for urban redevelopment.

Under such conditions people must end up in total anomie, with no meaningful relation to the environment and society. There seem to be two alternative remedies. One was proposed forty years ago by Le Corbusier: to centralize and homogenize completely, so that one dwelling place is exactly like another, with identical furniture, services, and surroundings. When all live in identical hotel rooms, mobility does not involve much dislocation. The other alternative is to build communities where meaningful voluntary association is again possible; that is, to decentralize. This has, of course, been the wistful aim of suburbanism, and it continually appears in the real-estate advertisements. But a suburb is not a decentralist community; its purposes, way of life, and decisions are determined by business headquarters, the national standard of living, and the bureau of highways. The hope of community is in people deciding important matters for themselves.

VII

A student raises a related objection: Decentralism is for small towns; it cannot work with big, dense populations. But I don't think this objection has any merit. Decentralism is a kind of social organization; it does not involve geographical isolation, but a particular sociological use of geography.

In important respects, a city of five million can be decentrally organized as many scores of unique communities in the framework of a busy metropolis.

Usually in modern urban administration, the various municipal functions—school, job induction, social work, health, police and court for misdemeanors, post office, housing and rent control, election district, etc.—are divided into units only for the administrative convenience of City Hall. The districts do not coincide with one another or with neighborhoods. A citizen with business or complaint must seek out the district office of each department, or perhaps go to City Hall. And correspondingly, there is no possible forum to discuss the coordination of the various functions except at the very top, with the Mayor or before the City Council.

Decentralist organization would rather follow the actuality of living in an urban community, where housing, schooling, shopping, policing, social services, politics are integrally related. Each neighborhood should have a local City Hall. Such *arrondissements* could have considerable autonomy within the municipal administration that controls transit, sanitation, museums, etc., whatever is necessarily or conveniently centralized. Taxes could be collected centrally and much of the take divided among the neighborhoods to be budgeted locally.

For the average citizen, the convergence of all kinds of related business in one local center is not only convenient but must lead to more acquaintance and involvement. Poor people especially do not know their way around, are stymied by forms to fill out, and have no professional help; they are defeated by fighting City Hall and soon give up. Besides, each neighborhood has interlocking problems peculiar to itself. These can be reasonably confronted by citizens and local officials, but they are lost in the inner politics of central bureaucracies that have quite different axes to grind.

For instance, a neighborhood so constituted might learn to decide on its own redevelopment. In programs for urban renewal, the Federal government follows the traditional formula of balancing centralism and decentralism and asks for approval of plans by the local community. Cities therefore set up local "planning boards." But this works out as follows. Occasionally, middle-class residential neighborhoods can organize themselves to prevent any change whatever; poor people are entirely passive to the powers-that-be; most usually, the boards are rubber stamps for City Hall and promoters. The say of a neighborhood in its destiny can be meaningful only if the neighborhood has begun to be conscious of itself as a community. For this, mere "consent" or "participation" is not enough; there must be a measure of real initiating and deciding, grounded in acquaintance and trust.

However, the question is not whether decentralization can work in dense urban populations, but how to make it work, for it is imperative. The increase of urban social disease and urban mental disease is fundamentally due to powerlessness, resignation, and withdrawal, as if people's only way to assert vitality is to develop symptoms. The central authorities try to cope as stern or hygienic caretakers; the citizens respond by becoming "community-dependent"—in jail, in the hospital, on relief; that is, they become chronic patients. With many, this has gone on for two and three generations.

VIII

Yet something further needs to be said about big, dense populations. In my opinion, there is a limit of urban density and urban sprawl beyond which *no* form of social organization, centralist or decentralist, can cope. Urban crowding creates a peculiar climate of both too many social relations and a kind of sensory and emotional deprivation. Instead of contact and communication, there is noise and withdrawal. It is no different from John Calhoun's overcrowded rodents who become confused and die. It is as if the circuits are clogged. Similarly, Harrison Matthews has shown that many mammals who in the wild are peaceful, become hostile in the "urban conditions" of a zoo, where there is not enough "social space" to experiment with their territoriality and hierarchy. Another naturalist, Loren Eiseley, says, "The higher the human population mounts, the more humanity in its behavior resembles the jostlings of the molecules of a gas under confined circumstances. It is not out of such confinement that a truly human future can be assured." For instance, the density of population in Central Harlem, at 67,000 per square mile, is nearly three times that of New York City as a whole. Even apart from the other unfavorable conditions of the Negroes, such crowding itself is pathological, overstimulating yet culturally impoverishing, destructive of solitude, excessively and brutally policed.

Our degree of urbanization is beyond reason. In this country we have the symptoms of a "population explosion" at the same time that vast and beautiful rural regions have become depopulated. . . . In the present setup, only big operators with migrant labor can make a go of farming, and the farm subsidies work disproportionately in favor of this group. Except for a few earnest but powerless voices, there is a general agreement to let farming-as-a-way-of-life die out. Yet no effort whatever is made to find urban substitutes for the independence, multifarious skill, community spirit, and extended family that were rural values.

During the Great Depression, the Roosevelt Administration made some efforts to support subsistence farming, as a factor of social stability and to relieve both rural and urban misery. But with the return of Prosperity, nothing further came of it. (We shall refer again to the shaggy decentralism of parts of the early New Deal. . . .)

IX

A student hotly objects that decentralism is humanly unrealistic, it "puts too much faith in human nature" by relying on in-

trinsic motives, like interest in the job and voluntary association. Another student mentions Rousseau, who is still aca-
demically out of fashion since his debunking by Professor
Babbitt a generation ago. (Jefferson, too, is now getting his
lumps.)

This objection is remarkably off-base. My experience is that
most decentralists are crotchety and skeptical and tend rather to
follow Aristotle than Rousseau. We must avoid concentration of
power precisely because we *are* fallible; *quis custodiet cus-
todes?* Democracy, Aristotle says, is to be preferred because it
is the "least evil" form of government, since it divides power
among many. I think the student states the moral issue upside
down. The moral question is not whether men are "good
enough" for a type of social organization but whether the type
of organization is useful to develop the potentialities of intelligence, grace, and freedom in men.

More deeply, the distrust of "human nature," of course, is
anxious conformism. One must save face, not make a mistake
in any detail; so one clings to an assigned role. But, unfortunately, the bigger the organization, the more face to save.
For instance, we shall see that the government Peace Corps
is many times as expensive as similar less official operations
largely because an errant twenty-year-old well-digger might become an International Incident, so one cannot be too careful
in selecting him. Convenience of supervision overrides performance. And the more "objective" the better. If the punch
card approves, no one is guilty. To bureaucrats, a fatal hall-
mark of decentralist enterprises is their variety in procedure and
persons; how can one *know,* with a percentage validity, that
these methods and persons are *right?*

Morally, all styles of social organization are self-proving,
for people understand the rightness of what everybody in fact
does. But different styles have different norms. The centralizing style makes for both petty conforming and admiration for
bigness. The more routine and powerless people are, the more
they are mesmerized by extrinsic proofs of production and
power. An enterprise that is designed on a small scale for a

particular need of particular people comes to be regarded as though it were nothing at all. To win attention and support, it must call itself a Pilot Project, promising mighty applications.

Nevertheless, still deeper than these neurotic confusions, there is, in my opinion, an authentic confusion in the face of unprecedented conditions of modern times that makes for rigidity and fear of social experiment. A student says, "We could afford to experiment if it were not for the Chinese, the Cubans, the crime rate, the unemployment, the space race, the population explosion." The leap in technology, the galloping urbanization, nuclear weapons, the breakdown of the colonial system—all involve threats and dilemmas. The inevitable response of people is to rally to the style of strict control by experts. In emergencies, centralized organization seems to make sense and often does make sense. It is also comfortingly dictatorial.

X

Finally, the moral objection is stated also the opposite way: decentralizing is impossible, not because people are incapable but because the powers-that-be won't allow it. (This student is an Angry Young Man.) Granting that in some areas decentralization is workable, how could it possibly be brought about? We cannot expect central powers to delegate autonomy any more than we can expect the nation-states to give up any of their sovereignty and grandeur. Indeed, the tendency is entirely in the other direction, toward bigger corporations, combinations, and tie-ins, toward tighter scheduling and grading in education, toward increased standardization and the application of automatic and computer technology in every field, and of course toward the increase of power in Washington to become the greatest landlord, the greatest sponsor of research, and the greatest policeman.

Yes. But there are forces also in the opposite direction.

I must assume, for instance, that it is not a social accident that I, as an author, am writing this book.

In principle, there are two ways in which an overcentralized system can become more mixed. Voluntary associations form spontaneously because of pressing needs to which the central system is irrelevant or antipathetic. Or the central authority itself chooses, or is forced, to build in decentral parts because its method is simply not working.

There is a marked trend toward spontaneous associations that indicates first a despair of, and then an indifference to, the regular methods. One must "do it oneself." We have already noticed the spontaneity, localism, and decentralist federation of the Negro civil rights movement, as different from the more conventional maneuvering of the Urban League and the older NAACP. But this is part of a general spread of para-legal demonstrating, boycotting, and show of power that express dissent with formal procedures that are not effective. The great discovery has been nonviolent activism, and this is peculiarly epidemic, for it immediately provides something to do rather than merely being balked—a beautiful feature of it, often, is to balk the authorities who have been balking us; yet it does not require forming political parties or organizing private armies. (When nonviolence is morally authentic, indeed, its very action is decentralizing: it restores the opposition to being persons rather than personnel. Violence has the contrary effect, of welding people into rigid organizations.)

Do-It-Yourself can be para-institutional if not overtly para-legal. Beat youth withdraws from the economy and tries to contrive a community culture of its own. Off-Broadway first withdraws from Broadway, dissident artists first withdraw from the big commercial galleries and set up their own galleries, etc.; but then there spreads a distaste for formal showings altogether. Students quit famous universities because they decide they are not being educated; then they form, for instance, the Northern Student Movement in order to tutor backward urban children; but then the Northern Student

Movement decides that the public school curriculum is inadequate, and the tutors will teach according to their own lights. Freedom Now sets up what amounts to a para-party in Mississippi.

And there is a similar tone even within the political framework. Contrasted with older "reform" movements which were devoted to purging the bosses and grafters, the new urban reform movements rapidly constitute themselves *ad hoc* for a concrete purpose other than getting hold of the party machinery, usually to block outrageous encroachments of government or big institutions. (Unfortunately, however, these reform "movements" usually do not have a counter-program; they stop with exercising a veto, lose steam, and eventually lose the original issue too. . . .

All this kind of ferment is what Arthur Waskow, of the Institute for Policy Studies, calls "creative disorder."

But also, as I shall spell out in the next chapter, the startling strength of know-nothing movements in the country is importantly due to justified dissatisfaction with the centralization, exactly as they claim when they reiterate the slogan, "Government must not do what people can do for themselves." By "people" our reactionary friends seem mainly to mean corporations, which are not people, yet I do not think that liberals and progressives pay attention to the underlying gripe, the loss of self-determination. The liberals glibly repeat that the complex problems of modern times do not allow simplistic solutions; no, they don't; but what is the use of "rational" solutions which finally are not the solutions of one's underlying problem?

XI

I do not notice any significant disposition of central powers to decentralize themselves. Rather, when the organization begins to creak, their disposition is to enlarge it further by adding new bureaus and overseers, to stall by appointing committees without power, to disregard difficulties and hope they will go away, or to call hard cases "deviant" and put them out of circulation.

Nevertheless, there are examples to show how decentralization *can* be built in.

The management of a giant corporation—General Motors is the classic example—can shrewdly decide to delegate a measure of autonomy to its corporate parts, because more flexible enterprising is more profitable in the long run. Similarly, a huge physical plant can be geographically dispersed, and the management somewhat decentralized, to save on labor costs and get better-tax breaks. In the Soviet Union, correspondingly, there is pressure for regional industrial councils, especially for allocating consumer goods. Naturally, these motives do nothing at all for the great majority of subordinates, though they multiply vice-presidents and local commissars.

More interesting for our purposes is the multifarious application of industrial psychology. For the most part, the pyschologists are decentralist by disposition and have taught a wisdom opposite to the time-motion studics of "scientific business management." Rather than subdividing the workman further and departmentalizing further, they have urged that it is efficient to allow more choice and leeway, to ask for suggestions from below, to increase "belonging." To give a typical example: In one plant it has been found more productive in the long run for half a dozen workmen to assemble a big lathe from beginning to end and have the satisfaction of seeing it carried away than to subdivide the operation on a line.

Needless to say, our industrial psychologists cannot pursue their instincts to the logical conclusion, workers' management. Yet questions of degree are *not* trivial. Consider the following example: In an area of England, it is traditional to work by a gang or collective contract. (This "Coventry system" has been studied by Professor Melman of Columbia.) A group of workmen agree to complete in a period a certain quantity of piecework, for which they are paid a sum of money divided equally. The capitalist provides the machinery and materials, but everything else—work rules, schedule, hiring—is left to group decision. The group may be half a dozen or a couple of thousand. Humanly, such an arrangement has extraordinary advantages. Men exchange jobs and acquire new skills; they adjust the schedule to their convenience or pleasures; they bring in and train apprentices; they invent labor-saving devices, which are to their own advantage; they cover for one another when sick or for special vacations.

Obviously such a system, so amazingly at variance with our minute top-down regulation, time-clock discipline, labor-union details, and competitive spirit, is hard to build into most of American industry. Yet where it would suit, it would make a profound difference. Where would it suit? How could it be tailored? How to get it put into effect?

Sometimes Federal or State agencies have to rely on decentralist organizations to make their own operations feasible. "Community developers" are sent in, e.g., by Mobilization for Youth; or just come in, like Saul Alinsky. State-aided housing involves developing Tenants' Councils to give the families a means of complaint against the sponsors and of petition to the State.

In the recent student disorders at Berkeley, there was a remarkable resurgence of initiative by the faculty, just to make communication again possible, for the Administration was obviously entirely out of touch. The faculty then sought to resume faculty control of student discipline, but as of this writing (December 1964) the Regents have refused this.

The occasional attempts at University reform, to alleviate the regimenting by the credits and grading machine, have been decentral structures like in-built honors colleges or the federation of small colleges instead of unlimited expansion. (But we have not yet come to the wisdom of breaking up the sixteen-year interlocked school system and offering alternative ways of growing up and different speeds for education.)

An attempt to build in decentralization has recently been

occurring in the New York public school system. Because of a combination of near-riots in poor neighborhoods, some spectacular run-of-the-mill scandals, and the post-sputnik spotlight on upgrading, a new and pretty good Board was appointed. Deciding that the system is overcentralized, these gentlemen have resuscitated twenty-five local districts—averaging more than forty thousand children each!—and appointed local boards with rather indefinite powers to serve as liaison to the neighborhoods. But unlike the case of the Urban Renewal Planning Boards mentioned above, the intention has been to delegate positive powers; and, anyway, the remarkably strong-minded body of people who have been appointed to the local school boards have declined to be rubber stamps. For a couple of years now, there has been a jockeying for position and power. The local boards are empowered to hold budget hearings and "suggest" allocation of money. What does this mean? Could they "suggest" to eliminate some of the curriculum and services and substitute others? Some local board members want to decentralize radically, making the field superintendents (with their advisory boards) nearly autonomous within the big system, as is reasonable, since different neighborhoods have different conditions and must therefore have different curricula, staff, and service needs.

One of the Manhattan boards, curious to know what its sister boards were doing, convened a meeting of the five Manhattan boards, and they agreed to exchange minutes. At once central headquarters protested and forbade such attempts at federation. "If you issue joint statements," headquarters pointed out, "people will think that you speak for the school system." "What can you do about it?" asked the locals; "since you have called us into existence, we exist, and since we exist, we intend to act." I mention this incident not because it is important in itself, but because it is at the heart of the constitutional problem of centralization and decentralization.

These, then, are the chief *prima facie* objections raised by college students. Decentralization is disorderly and "anarchic." You cannot decentralize air-traffic control and public health. What about automation? Decentralization is a peasant ideology. It makes for "States' Rights" injustice. It is unworkable with big, dense populations. It implies an unrealistic faith that human nature is good and human beings are reasonable. It is impossible to go against the overwhelming trend toward bigness and power.

What is most discouraging in such discussions is that students keep referring to "your system" or "the decentralist system."

But I am not proposing a system. It is hard to convince college students that it is improbable that there *could* be a single appropriate style of organization or economy to fit all the functions of society, anymore than there could—or ought to be—a single mode of education, "going to school," that suits almost everybody, or anymore than there is a "normal" psychology that is healthy for almost everybody.

Rather, it seems to me as follows. We are in a period of excessive centralization. In this book I shall try to demonstrate that in many functions this style is economically inefficient, technologically unnecessary, and humanly damaging. Therefore we might adopt a political *maxim:* to decentralize where, how, and how much is expedient. But where, how, and how much are *empirical* questions. They require research and experiment.

In the existing overcentralized climate of opinion, it is just this research and experiment that we are not getting. Among all the departments, agencies, and commissions in Washington, I have not heard of one that deals with the organizational *style* of municipalities, social work, manufacturing, merchandising, or education in terms of technical and economic efficiency and effect on persons. Therefore, I urge students who are going on to graduate work to choose their theses in this field.

7. Repressive Tolerance

HERBERT MARCUSE

This essay examines the idea of tolerance in our advanced industrial society. The conclusion reached is that the realization of the objective of tolerance would call for intolerance toward prevailing policies, attitudes, opinions, and the extension of tolerance to policies, attitudes, and opinions which are outlawed or suppressed. In other words, today tolerance appears again as what it was in its origins, at the beginning of the modern period—a partisan goal, a subversive liberating notion and practice. Conversely, what is proclaimed and practiced as tolerance today, is in many of its most effective manifestations serving the cause of oppression.

From *A Critique of Pure Tolerance,* ed. Robert Paul Wolff, Barrington Moore, Jr., and Herbert Marcuse (Boston: Beacon Press, 1965), pp. 81–123. Copyright © 1965, 1969 by Herbert Marcuse. Reprinted by permission of the author and publisher. *Author's note:* This essay is dedicated to my students at Brandeis University.

self-imposed) limitations is intensified. Generally, the function and value of tolerance depend on the equality prevalent in the society in which tolerance is practiced. Tolerance itself stands subject to overriding criteria: its range and its limits cannot be defined in terms of the respective society. In other words, tolerance is an end in itself only when it is truly universal, practiced by the rulers as well as by the ruled, by the lords as well as by the peasants, by the sheriffs as well as by their victims. And such universal tolerance is possible only when no real or alleged enemy requires in the national interest the education and training of people in military violence and destruction. As long as these conditions do not prevail, the conditions of tolerance are "loaded": they are determined and defined by the institutionalized inequality (which is certainly compatible with constitutional equality), i.e., by the class structure of society. In such a society, tolerance is *de facto* limited on the dual ground of legalized violence or suppression (police, armed forces, guards of all sorts) and of the privileged position held by the predominant interests and their "connections."

These background limitations of tolerance are normally prior to the explicit and judicial limitations as defined by the courts, custom, governments, etc. (for example, "clear and present danger," threat to national security, heresy). Within the framework of such a social structure, tolerance can be safely practiced and proclaimed. It is of two kinds: (1) the passive toleration of entrenched and established attitudes and ideas even if their damaging effect on man and nature is evident; and (2) the active, official tolerance granted to the Right as well as to the Left, to movements of aggression as well as to movements of peace, to the party of hate as well as to that of humanity. I call this nonpartisan tolerance "abstract" or "pure" inasmuch as it refrains from taking sides— but in doing so it actually protects the already established machinery of discrimination.

The tolerance which enlarged the range and content of freedom was always partisan—intolerant toward the protagonists of the repressive status quo. The issue was only the degree and extent of intolerance. In the firmly established liberal society of England and the United States, freedom of speech and assembly was granted even to the radical enemies of society, provided they did not make the transition from word to deed, from speech to action.

Relying on the effective background limitations imposed by its class structure, the society seemed to practice general tolerance. But liberalist theory had already placed an important condition on tolerance: it was "to apply only to human beings in the maturity of their faculties." John Stuart Mill does not only speak of children and minors; he elaborates: "Liberty, as a principle, has no application to any state of things anterior to the time when mankind have become capable of being improved by free and equal discussion." Anterior to that time, men may still be barbarians, and "despotism is a legitimate mode of government in dealing with barbarians, provided the end be their improvement, and the means justified by actually effecting that end." Mill's often-quoted words have a less familiar implication on which their meaning depends: the internal connection between liberty and truth. There is a sense in which truth is the end of liberty, and liberty must be defined and confined by truth. Now in what sense can liberty be for the sake of truth? Liberty is self-determination, autonomy—this is almost a tautology, but a tautology which results from a whole series of synthetic judgments. It stipulates the ability to determine one's own life: to be able to determine what to do and what not to do, what to suffer and what not. But the subject of this autonomy is never the contingent, private individual as that which he actually is or happens to be; it is rather the individual as a human being who is capable of being free with the others. And the problem of making possible such a harmony between every individual liberty and the other is not that of finding a compromise between competitors, or between freedom and law, between general and individual interest, common and private welfare in an *established* society, but of *creat-*

ing the society in which man is no longer enslaved by institutions which vitiate self-determination from the beginning. In other words, freedom is still to be created even for the freest of the existing societies. And the direction in which it must be sought, and the institutional and cultural changes which may help to attain the goal are, at least in developed civilization, *comprehensible,* that is to say, they can be identified and projected, on the basis of experience, by human reason.

In the interplay of theory and practice, true and false solutions become distinguishable—never with the evidence of necessity, never as the positive, only with the certainty of a reasoned and reasonable chance, and with the persuasive force of the negative. For the true positive is the society of the future and therefore beyond definition and determination, while the existing positive is that which must be surmounted. But the experience and understanding of the existent society may well be capable of identifying what is *not* conducive to a free and rational society, what impedes and distorts the possibilities of its creation. Freedom is liberation, a specific historical process in theory and practice, and as such it has its right and wrong, its truth and falsehood.

The uncertainty of chance in this distinction does not cancel the historical objectivity, but it necessitates freedom of thought and expression as preconditions of finding the way to freedom—it necessitates *tolerance.* However, this tolerance cannot be indiscriminate and equal with respect to the contents of expression, neither in word nor in deed; it cannot protect false words and wrong deeds which demonstrate that they contradict and counteract the possibilities of liberation. Such indiscriminate tolerance is justified in harmless debates, in conversation, in academic discussion; it is indispensable in the scientific enterprise, in private religion. But society cannot be indiscriminate where the pacification of existence, where freedom and happiness themselves are at stake: here, certain things cannot be said, certain ideas cannot be expressed, certain policies cannot be proposed, certain behavior cannot be permitted without making tolerance an instrument for the continuation of servitude.

The danger of "destructive tolerance" (Baudelaire), of "benevolent neutrality" toward *art* has been recognized: the market, which absorbs equally well (although with often quite sudden fluctuations) art, anti-art, and non-art, all possible conflicting styles, schools, forms, provides a "complacent receptacle, a friendly abyss" (Edgar Wind, *Art and Anarchy* [New York: Knopf, 1964], p. 101) in which the radical impact of art, the protest of art against the established reality is swallowed up. However, censorship of art and literature is regressive under all circumstances. The authentic oeuvre is not and cannot be a prop of oppression, and pseudo-art (which can be such a prop) is not art. Art stands against history, withstands history which has been the history of oppression, for art subjects reality to laws other than the established ones to the laws of the Form which creates a different reality—negation of the established one even where art depicts the established reality. But in its struggle with history, art subjects itself to history: history enters the definition of art and enters into the distinction between art and pseudo-art. Thus it happens that what was once art becomes pseudo-art. Previous forms, styles, and qualities, previous modes of protest and refusal cannot be recaptured in or against a different society. There are cases where an authentic oeuvre carries a regressive political message—Dostoevski is a case in point. But then, the message is canceled by the oeuvre itself: the regressive political content is absorbed, *aufgehoben* in the artistic form: in the work as literature.

Tolerance of free speech is the way of improvement, of progress in liberation, *not* because there is no objective truth, and improvement must necessarily be a compromise between a variety of opinions, but because there *is* an objective truth which can be discovered, ascertained only in learning and comprehending that which is and that which can be and ought to be done for the sake of improving the lot of mankind.

This common and historical "ought" is not immediately evident, at hand: it has to be uncovered by "cutting through," "splitting," "breaking asunder" (*dis-cutio*) the given material —separating right and wrong, good and bad, correct and incorrect. The subject whose "improvement" depends on a progressive historical practice is each man as man, and this universality is reflected in that of the discussion, which a priori does not exclude any group or individual. But even the all-inclusive character of liberalist tolerance was, at least in theory, based on the proposition that men were (potential) *individuals* who could learn to hear and see and feel by themselves, to develop their own thoughts, to grasp their true interests and rights and capabilities, also against established authority and opinion. This was the rationale of free speech and assembly. Universal toleration becomes questionable when its rationale no longer prevails, when tolerance is administered to manipulated and indoctrinated individuals who parrot, as their own, the opinion of their masters, for whom heteronomy has become autonomy.

The telos of tolerance is truth. It is clear from the historical record that the authentic spokesmen of tolerance had more and other truth in mind than that of propositional logic and academic theory. John Stuart Mill speaks of the truth which is persecuted in history and which does *not* triumph over persecution by virtue of its "inherent power," which in fact has no inherent power "against the dungeon and the stake." And he enumerates the "truths" which were cruelly and successfully liquidated in the dungeons and at the stake: that of Arnold of Brescia, of Fra Dolcino, of Savonarola, of the Albigensians, Waldensians, Lollards, and Hussites. Tolerance is first and foremost for the sake of the heretics—the historical road toward *humanitas* appears as heresy: target of persecution by the powers that be. Heresy by itself, however, is no token of truth.

The criterion of progress in freedom according to which Mill judges these movements is the Reformation. The evaluation is *ex post,* and his list includes opposites (Savonarola too would have burned Fra Dolcino). Even the ex post evaluation is contestable as to its truth: history corrects the judgment—too late. The correction does not help the victims and does not absolve their executioners. However, the lesson is clear: intolerance has delayed progress and has prolonged the slaughter and torture of innocents for hundreds of years. Does this clinch the case for indiscriminate, "pure" tolerance? Are there historical conditions in which such toleration impedes liberation and multiplies the victims who are sacrified to the status quo? Can the indiscriminate guaranty of political rights and liberties be repressive? Can such tolerance serve to contain qualitative social change?

I shall discuss this question only with reference to political movements, attitudes, schools of thought, philosophies which are "political" in the widest sense—affecting the society as a whole, demonstrably transcending the sphere of privacy. Moreover, I propose a shift in the focus of the discussion: it will be concerned not only, and not primarily, with tolerance toward radical extremes, minorities, subversives, etc., but rather with tolerance toward majorities, toward official and public opinion, toward the established protectors of freedom. In this case, the discussion can have as a frame of reference only a democratic society, in which the people, as individuals and as members of political and other organizations, participate in the making, sustaining, and changing of policies. In an authoritarian system, the people do not tolerate—they suffer established policies.

Under a system of constitutionally guaranteed and (generally and without too many and too glaring exceptions) practiced civil rights and liberties, opposition and dissent are tolerated unless they issue in violence and/or in exhortation to and organization of violent subversion. The underlying assumption is that the established society is free, and that any improvement, even a change in the social structure and social values, would come about in the normal course of events, prepared, defined, and tested in free and equal discussion, on the

open marketplace of ideas and goods.* Now in recalling
John Stuart Mill's passage, I drew attention to the premise
hidden in this assumption: free and equal discussion can fulfill
the function attributed to it only if it is *rational*—expression
and development of independent thinking, free from indoctrination, manipulation, extraneous authority. The notion of
pluralism and countervailing powers is no sutstitute for this requirement. One might in theory construct a state in which a
multitude of different pressures, interests, and authorities balance each other out and result in a truly general and rational
interest. However, such a construct badly fits a society in which
powers are and ramain unequal and even increase their unequal weight when they run their own course. It fits even
worse when the variety of pressures unifies and coagulates into
an overwhelming whole, integrating the particular countervailing powers by virtue of an increasing standard of living and an
increasing concentration of power. Then, the laborer, whose
real interest conflicts with that of management, the common
consumer whose real interest conflicts with that of the pro-
ducer, the intellectual whose vocation conflicts with that of his
employer find themselves submitting to a system against which
they are powerless and appear unreasonable. The ideas of the
available alternatives evaporates into an utterly utopian dimension in which it is at home, for a free society, is indeed un-
realistically and undefinably different from the existing ones.
Under these circumstances, whatever improvement may occur
"in the normal course of events" and without subversion is
likely to be improvement in the direction determined by the
particular interests which control the whole.

By the same token, those minorities which strive for a
change of the whole itself will, under optimal conditions which

* I wish to reiterate for the following discussion that, *de facto*,
tolerance is *not* indiscriminate and "pure" even in the most democratic
society. The "background limitations" stated on pages 141–142 restrict
tolerance before it begins to operate. The antagonistic structure of society
rigs the rules of the game. Those who stand against the established system are a priori at a disadvantage, which is not removed by the toleration of their ideas, speeches, and newspapers.

rarely prevail, be left free to deliberate and discuss, to speak and to assemble—and will be left harmless and helpless in the face of the overwhelming majority, which militates against qualitative social change. This majority is firmly grounded in the increasing satisfaction of needs, and technological and mental coordination, which testify to the general helplessness of radical groups in a well-functioning social system.

Within the affluent democracy, the affluent discussion prevails, and within the established framework, it is tolerant to a large extent. All points of view can be heard: the Communist and the Fascist, the Left and the Right, the white and the Negro, the crusaders for armament and for disarmament. Moreover, in endlessly dragging debates over the media, the stupid opinion is treated with the same respect as the intelligent one, the misinformed may talk as long as the informed, and propaganda rides along with education, truth with falsehood. This pure toleration of sense and nonsense is justified by the democratic argument that nobody, neither group nor individual, is in possession of the truth and capable of defining what is right and wrong, good and bad. Therefore, all contesting opinions must be submitted to "the people" for its deliberation and choice. But I have already suggested that the democratic argument implies a necessary condition, namely, that the people must be capable of deliberating and choosing on the basis of knowledge, that they must have access to authentic information, and that, on this basis, their evaluation must be the result of autonomous thought.

In the contemporary period, the democratic argument for abstract tolerance tends to be invalidated by the invalidation of the democratic process itself. The liberating force of democracy was the chance it gave to effective dissent, on the individual as well as social scale, its openness to qualitatively different forms of government, of culture, education, work—of the human existence in general. The toleration of free discussion and the equal right of opposites was to define and clarify the different forms of dissent: their direction, content, prospect. But with the concentration of economic and

political power and the integration of opposites in a society
which uses technology as an instrument of domination, effective dissent is blocked where it could freely emerge: in the
formation of opinion, in information and communication, in
speech and assembly. Under the rule of monopolistic media—
themselves the mere instruments of economic and political
power—a mentality is created for which right and wrong, true
and false are predefined wherever they affect the vital interests of the society. This is, prior to all expression and
communication, a matter of semantics: the blocking of effective dissent, of the recognition of that which is not of the
Establishment which begins in the language that is publicized
and administered. The meaning of words is rigidly stabilized.
Rational persuasion, persuasion to the opposite is all but
precluded. The avenues of entrance are closed to the meaning
of words and ideas other than the established one—established by the publicity of the powers that be, and verified in
their practices. Other words can be spoken and heard, other
ideas can be expressed, but, at the massive scale of the conservative majority (outside such enclaves as the intelligentsia),
they are immediately "evaluated" (i.e., automatically understood) in terms of the public language—a language which
determines "a priori" the direction in which the thought process moves. Thus the process of reflection ends where it
started: in the given conditions and relations. Self-validating,
the argument of the discussion repels the contradiction because the antithesis is redefined in terms of the thesis. For
example, thesis: we work for peace; antithesis: we prepare
for war (or even: we wage war); unification of opposites:
preparing for war *is* working for peace. Peace is redefined
as necessarily, in the prevailing situation, including preparation
for war (or even war) and in this Orwellian form, the meaning of the word "peace" is stabilized. Thus, the basic vocabulary of the Orwellian language operates as a priori categories of understanding: preforming all content. These conditions invalidate the logic of tolerance which involves the
rational development of meaning and precludes the closing of

meaning. Consequently, persuasion through discussion and the equal presentation of opposites (even where it is really equal) easily lose their liberating force as factors of understanding and learning; they are far more likely to strengthen the established thesis and to repel the alternatives.

Impartiality to the utmost, equal treatment of competing and conflicting issues is indeed a basic requirement for decision-making in the democratic process—it is an equally basic requirement for defining the limits of tolerance. But in a democracy with totalitarian organization, objectivity may fulfill a very different function, namely, to foster a mental attitude which tends to obliterate the difference between true and false, information and indoctrination, right and wrong. In fact, the decision between opposed opinions has been made before the presentation and discussion get under way—made, not by a conspiracy or a sponsor or a publisher, not by any dictatorship, but rather by the "normal course of events," which is the course of administered events, and by the mentality shaped in this course. Here, too, it is the whole which determines the truth. Then the decision asserts itself, without any open violation of objectivity, in such things as the make-up of a newspaper (with the breaking up of vital information into bits interspersed between extraneous material, irrelevant items, relegating of some radically negative news to an obscure place), in the juxtaposition of gorgeous ads with unmitigated horrors, in the introduction and interruption of the broadcasting of facts by overwhelming commercials. The result is a *neutralization* of opposites, a neutralization, however, which takes place on the firm grounds of the structural limitation of tolerance and within a preformed mentality. When a magazine prints side by side a negative and a positive report on the FBI, it fulfills honestly the requirements of objectivity: however, the chances are that the positive wins because the image of the institution is deeply engraved in the mind of the people. Or, if a newscaster reports the torture and murder of civil rights workers in the same unemotional tone he uses to describe the stockmarket or the weather, or with the same great emotion with which he says his commercials, then such objectivity is spurious—more, it offends against humanity and truth by being calm where one should be enraged, by refraining from accusation where accusation is in the facts themselves. The tolerance expressed in such impartiality serves to minimize or even absolve prevailing intolerance and suppression. If objectivity has anything to do with truth, and if truth is more than a matter of logic and science, then this kind of objectivity is false and this kind of tolerance inhuman. And if it is necessary to break the established universe of meaning (and the practice enclosed in this universe) in order to enable man to find out what is true and false, this deceptive impartiality would have to be abandoned. The people exposed to this impartiality are no *tabulae rasae*, they are indoctrinated by the conditions under which they live and think and which they do not transcend. To enable them to become autonomous, to find by themselves what is true and what is false for man in the existing society, they would have to be freed from the prevailing indoctrination (which is no longer recognized as indoctrination). But this means that the trend would have to be reversed: they would have to get information slanted in the opposite direction. For the facts are never given immediately and never accessible immediately; they are established, "mediated" by those who made them; the truth, "the whole truth" surpasses these facts and requires the rupture with their appearance. This rupture— prerequisite and token of all freedom of thought and of speech—cannot be accomplished within the established framework of abstract tolerance and spurious objectivity because these are precisely the factors which precondition the mind *against* the rupture.

II

The factual barriers which totalitarian democracy erects against the efficacy of qualitative dissent are weak and pleasant enough compared with the practices of a dictatorship which claims to educate the people in the truth. With all its limitations and distortions, democratic tolerance is under all circumstances more humane than an institutionalized intolerance which sacrifices the rights and liberties of the living generations for the sake of future generations. The question is whether this is the only alternative. I shall presently try to suggest the direction in which an answer may be sought. In any case, the contrast is not between democracy in the abstract and dictatorship in the abstract.

Democracy is a form of government which fits very different types of society (this holds true even for a democracy with universal suffrage and equality before the law), and the human costs of a democracy are always and everywhere those exacted by the society whose government it is. Their range extends all the way from normal exploitation, poverty, and insecurity to the victims of wars, police actions, military aid, etc., in which the society is engaged—and not only to the victims within its own frontiers. These considerations can never justify the exacting of different sacrifices and different victims on behalf of a future better society, but they do allow weighing the costs involved in the perpetuation of an existing society against the risk of promoting alternatives which offer a reasonable chance of pacification and liberation. Surely, no government can be expected to foster its own subversion, but in a democracy such a right is vested in the people (i.e., in the majority of the people). This means that the ways should not be blocked on which a subversive majority could develop, and if they are blocked by organized repression and indoctrination, their reopening may require apparently undemocratic means. They would include the withdrawal of toleration of speech and assembly from groups and movements which promote aggressive policies, armament, chauvinism, discrimination on the grounds of race and religion, or which oppose the extension of public services, social security, medical care, etc. Moreover, the restoration of freedom of thought may necessitate new and rigid restrictions on teachings and practices in the educational institutions which, by their very methods and concepts, serve to enclose the mind within the established universe of discourse and behavior—thereby precluding a priori a rational evaluation of the alternatives. And to the degree to which freedom of thought involves the struggle against inhumanity, restoration of such freedom would also imply intolerance toward scientific research in the interest of deadly "deterrents," of abnormal human endurance under inhuman conditions, etc. I shall presently discuss the question as to who is to decide on the distinction between liberating and repressive, human and inhuman teachings and practices; I have already suggested that this distinction is not a matter of value-preference but of rational criteria.

While the reversal of the trend in the educational enterprise at least could conceivably be enforced by the students and teachers themselves, and thus be self-imposed, the systematic withdrawal of tolerance toward regressive and repressive opinions and movements could only be envisaged as results of large-scale pressure which would amount to an upheaval. In other words, it would presuppose that which is still to be accomplished: the reversal of the trend. However, resistance at particular occasions, boycott, nonparticipation at the local and small-group level may perhaps prepare the ground. The subversive character of the restoration of freedom appears most clearly in that dimension of society where false tolerance and free enterprise do perhaps the most serious and lasting damage, namely, in business and publicity. Against the emphatic insistence on the part of spokesmen for labor, I maintain that practices such as planned obsolescence, collusion between union leadership and management, slanted publicity are not simply imposed from above on a powerless rank and file, but are *tolerated* by them—and by the consumer at large. However, it would be ridiculous to speak of a possible withdrawal of tolerance with respect to these practices and to the ideologies promoted by them. For they pertain to the basis on which the repressive affluent society rests and reproduces itself and its vital defenses—their removal would be that total revolution which this society so effectively repels.

To discuss tolerance in such a society means to re-examine the issue of violence and the traditional distinction between violent and non-violent action. The discussion should not, from the beginning, be clouded by ideologies which serve the perpetuation of violence. Even in the advanced centers of civilization, violence actually prevails: it is practiced by the police, in the prisons and mental institutions, in the fight against racial minorities; it is carried, by the defenders of metropolitan freedom, into the backward countries. This violence indeed breeds violence. But to refrain from violence in the face of vastly superior violence is one thing, to renounce a priori violence against violence, on ethical or psychological grounds (because it may antagonize sympathizers) is another. Nonviolence is normally not only preached to but exacted from the weak—it is a necessity rather than a virtue, and normally it does not seriously harm the case of the strong. (Is the case of India an exception? There, passive resistance was carried through on a massive scale, which disrupted, or threatened to disrupt, the economic life of the country. Quantity turns into quality: on such a scale, passive resistance is no longer passive—it ceases to be nonviolent. The same holds true for the General Strike.) Robespierre's distinction between the terror of liberty and the terror of despotism, and his moral glorification of the former belongs to the most convincingly condemned aberrations, even if the white terror was more bloody than the red terror. The comparative evaluation in terms of the number of victims is the quantifying approach which reveals the man-made horror throughout history that made violence a necessity. In terms of historical function, there is a difference between revolutionary and reactionary violence, between violence practiced by the oppressed and by the oppressors. In terms of ethics, both forms of violence are inhuman and evil—but since when is history made in accordance with ethical standards? To start applying them at the point where the oppressed rebel against the oppressors, the have-nots against the haves, is serving the cause of actual violence by weakening the protest against it.

Comprenez enfin ceci: si la violence a commencé ce soir, si l'exploitation ni l'opression n'ont jamais existé sur terre, peut-être la non-violence affichée peut apaiser la querelle. Mais si le régime tout entier et jusqu'á vos nonviolentes pensées sont conditionnées par une oppression millénaire, votre passivité ne sert qu'à vous ranger du côté des oppresseurs. (Sartre, Preface to Frantz Fanon, *Les Damnés de la Terre*, Paris: Maspéro, 1961, p. 22.)

The very notion of false tolerance, and the distinction between right and wrong limitations on tolerance, between progressive and regressive indoctrination, revolutionary and reactionary violence demand the statement of criteria for its validity. These standards must be prior to whatever constitutional and legal criteria are set up and applied in an existing society (such as "clear and present danger," and other established definitions of civil rights and liberties), for such definitions themselves presuppose standards of freedom and repression as applicable or not applicable in the respective society: they are specifications of more general concepts. By whom, and according to what standards, can the political distinction between true and false, progressive and regressive (for in this sphere, these pairs are equivalent) be made and its validity be justified? At the outset, I propose that the question cannot be answered in terms of the alternative between democracy and dictatorship, according to which, in the latter, one individual or group, without any effective control from below, arrogate to themselves the decision. Historically, even in the most democratic democracies, the vital and final decisions affecting the society as a whole have been made, constitutionally or in fact, by one or several groups without effective control by the people themselves. The ironical question: who educated the educators (i.e., the political leaders) also applies to democracy. The only authentic alternative and negation of dictatorship (with respect to this question) would be a society in which "the people" have become autonomous individuals, freed from the repressive requirements of a struggle for existence in the interest of domination, and as such human beings choosing their government and determining their life. Such a society does not yet exist anywhere. In the meantime, the question must be treated *in abstracto*—abstraction, not from the historical possibilities, but from the realities of the prevailing societies.

I suggested that the distinction between true and false tolerance, between progress and regression can be made rationally on empirical grounds. The real possibilities of human freedom are relative to the attained stage of civilization. They depend on the material and intellectual resources available at the respective stage, and they are quantifiable and calculable to a high degree. So are, at the sage of advanced industrial society, the most rational ways of using these resources and distributing the social product with priority on the satisfaction of vital needs and with a minimum of toil and injustice. In other words, it is possible to define the direction in which prevailing institutions, policies, opinions would have to be changed in order to improve the chance of a peace which is not identical with cold war and a little hot war, and a satisfaction of needs which does not feed on poverty, oppression, and exploitation. Consequently, it is also possible to identify policies, opinions, movements which would promote this chance, and those which would do the opposite. Suppression of the regressive ones is a prerequisite for the strengthening of the progressive ones.

The question, who is qualified to make all these distinctions, definitions, identifications for the society as a whole, has now one logical answer, namely, everyone "in the maturity of his faculties" as a human being, everyone who has learned to think rationally and autonomously. The answer to Plato's educational dictatorship is the democratic educational dictatorship of free men. John Stuart Mill's conception of the *res publica* is not the opposite of Plato's: the liberal too demands the authority of Reason not only as an intellectual but also as a political power. In Plato, rationality is confined to the small number of philosopher-kings; in Mill, every rational human being participates in the discussion and decision—but only as a rational being. Where society has entered the phase of total administration and indoctrination, this would be a small number indeed, and not necessarily that of the elected representatives of the people. The problem is not that of an educational dictatorship, but that of breaking the tyranny of public opinion and its makers in the closed society.

However, granted the empirical rationality of the distinction between progress and regression, and granted that it may be applicable to tolerance, and may justify strongly discriminatory tolerance on political grounds (cancellation of the liberal creed of free and equal discussion), another impossible consequence would follow. I said that, by virtue of its inner logic, withdrawal of tolerance from regressive movements and discriminatory tolerance in favor of progressive tendencies would be tantamount to the "official" promotion of subversion. The historical calculus of progress (which is actually the calculus of the prospective reduction of cruelty, misery, suppression) seems to involve the calculated choice between two forms of political violence: that on the part of the legally constituted powers (by their legitimate action, or by their tacit consent, or by their inability to prevent violence) and that on the part of potentially subversive movements. Moreover, with respect to the latter, a policy of unequal treatment would protect radicalism on the Left against that on the Right. Can the historical calculus be reasonably extended to the justification of one form of violence as against another? Or better (since "justification" carries a moral connotation), is there historical evidence to the effect that the social origin and impetus of violence (from among the ruled or the ruling classes, the have or the have-nots, the Left or the Right) is in a demonstrable relation to progress (as defined above)?

With all the qualifications of a hypothesis based on an "open" historical record, it seems that the violence emanating from the rebellion of the oppressed classes broke the historical continuum of injustice, cruelty, and silence for a brief moment, brief but explosive enough to achieve an increase in the scope of freedom and justice, and a better and more equitable distribution of misery and oppression in a new social system—in one word: progress in civilization. The English civil wars, the French Revolution, the Chinese and the Cuban Revolutions may illustrate the hypothesis. In contrast, the one historical change from one social system to another, marking the beginning of a new period in civilization, which was *not* sparked and driven by an effective movement "from below," namely, the collapse of the Roman Empire in the West, brought about a long period of regression for long centuries, until a new, higher period of civilization was painfully born in the violence of the heretic revolts of the thirteenth century and in the peasant and laborer revolts of the fourteenth century.[1]

With respect to historical violence emanating from among ruling classes, no such relation to progress seems to obtain. The long series of dynastic and imperialist wars, the liquidation of Spartacus in Germany in 1919, Fascism and Nazism did not break but rather tightened and streamlined the continuum of suppression. I said emanating "from among ruling classes": to be sure, there is hardly any organized violence from above that does not mobilize and activate mass support from below; the decisive question is, on behalf of and in the interest of which groups and institutions is such violence released? And the answer is not necessarily ex post: in the historical examples just mentioned, it could be and was anticipated whether the movement would serve the revamping of the old order or the emergence of the new.

Liberating tolerance, then, would mean intolerance against movements from the Right, and toleration of movements from the Left. As to the scope of this tolerance and intolerance: ... it would extend to the stage of action as well as of discussion and propaganda, of deed as well as of word. The traditional criterion of clear and present danger seems no longer adequate to a stage where the whole society is in the situation of the theater audience when somebody cries "fire."

It is a situation in which the total catastrophy could be triggered off any moment, not only by a technical error, but also by a rational miscalculation of risks, or by a rash speech of one of the leaders. In past and different circumstances, the speeches of the Fascist and Nazi leaders were the immediate prologue to the massacre. The distance between the propaganda and the action, between the organization and its release on the people had become too short. But the spreading of the word could have been stopped before it was too late: if democratic tolerance had been withdrawn when the future leaders started their campaign, mankind would have had a chance of avoiding Auschwitz and a World War.

The whole post-fascist period is one of clear and present danger. Consequently, true pacification requires the withdrawal of tolerance before the deed, at the stage of communication in word, print, and picture. Such extreme suspension of the right of free speech and free assembly is indeed justified only if the whole of society is in extreme danger. I maintain that our society is in such an emergency situation, and that it has become the normal state of affairs. Different opinions and "philosophies" can no longer compete peacefully for adherence and persuasion on rational grounds: the "marketplace of ideas" is organized and delimited by those who determine the national and the individual interest. In this society, for which the ideologists have proclaimed the "end of ideology," the false consciousness has become the general consciousness—from the government down to its last objects. The small and powerless minorities which struggle against the false consciousness and its beneficiaries must be helped: their continued existence is more important than the preservation of abused rights and liberties which grant constitutional powers to those who oppress these minorities. It should be evident by now that the exercise of civil rights by those who don't have them presupposes the withdrawal of civil rights from those who prevent their exercise, and that liberation of the Damned of the Earth presupposes suppression not only of their old but also of their new masters.

Withdrawal of tolerance from regressive movements *before* they can become active, intolerance even toward thought, opinion, and word, and finally, intolerance in the opposite direction, that is, toward the self-styled conservatives, to the political Right—these anti-democratic notions respond to the actual development of the democratic society which has destroyed the basis for universal tolerance. The conditions under which tolerance can again become a liberating and humanizing force have still to be created. When tolerance mainly serves the protection and preservation of a repressive society, when it serves to neutralize opposition and to render men immune against other and better forms of life, then tolerance has been perverted. And when this perversion starts in the mind of the individual, in his consciousness, his needs, when heteronomous interests occupy him before he can experience his servitude, then the efforts to counteract his dehumanization must begin at the place of entrance, there where the false consciousness takes form (or rather, is systematically formed)—it must begin with stopping the words and images which feed this consciousness. To be sure, this is censorship, even precensorship, but openly directed against the more or less hidden censorship that permeates the free media. Where the false consciousness has become prevalent in national and popular behavior, it translates itself almost immediately into practice: the safe distance between ideology and reality, repressive thought and repressive action, between the word of destruction and the deed of destruction is dangerously shortened. Thus, the break through the false consciousness may provide the Archimedean point for a larger emancipation—at an infinitesimally small spot, to be sure, but it is on the enlargement of such small spots that the chance of change depends.

The forces of emancipation cannot be identified with any social class which, by virtue of its material condition, is free from false consciousness. Today, they are hopelessly dispersed throughout the society, and the fighting minorities and isolated groups are often in opposition to their own leadership. In the society at large, the mental space for denial and reflection must first be recreated. Repulsed by the concreteness of the administered society, the effort of emancipation becomes "abstract"; it is reduced to facilitating the recognition of what is going on, to freeing language from the tyranny of the Orwellian syntax and logic, to developing the concepts that comprehend reality. More than ever, the proposition holds true that progress in freedom demands progress in the *consciousness* of freedom. Where the mind has been made into a subject-object of politics and policies, intellectual autonomy, the realm of "pure" thought has become a matter of *political education* (or rather: counter-education).

This means that previously neutral, value-free, formal aspects of learning and teaching now become, on their own grounds and in their own right, political: learning to know the facts, the whole truth, and to comprehend it is radical criticism throughout, intellectual subversion. In a world in which the human faculties and needs are arrested or perverted, autonomous thinking leads into a "perverted world": contradiction and counter-image of the established world of repression. And this contradiction is not simply stipulated, is not simply the product of confused thinking or phantasy, but is the logical development of the given, the existing world. To the degree to which this development is actually impeded by the sheer weight of a repressive society and the necessity of making a living in it, repression invades the academic enterprise itself, even prior to all restrictions on academic freedom. The preempting of the mind vitiates impartiality and objectivity: unless the student learns to think in the opposite direction, he will be inclined to place the facts into the predominant framework of values. Scholarship, i.e., the acquisition and communication of knowledge, prohibits the purification and isolation of facts from the context of the whole truth. An essential part of the latter is recognition of the frightening extent to which history was made and recorded by and for the victors, that is, the extent to which history was the development of oppression. And this oppression is in the facts themselves which it establishes; thus they themselves carry a negative value as part and aspect of their facticity. To treat the great crusades *against* humanity (like that against the Albigensians) with the same impartiality as the desperate struggles *for* humanity means neutralizing their opposite historical function, reconciling the executioners with their victims, distorting the record. Such spurious neutrality serves to reproduce acceptance of the dominion of the victors in the consciousness of man. Here, too, in the education of those who are not yet maturely integrated, in the mind of the young, the ground for liberating tolerance is still to be created.

Education offers still another example of spurious, abstract tolerance in the guise of concreteness and truth: it is epitomized in the concept of self-actualization. From the permissiveness of all sorts of license to the child to the constant psychological concern with the personal problems of the student, a large-scale movement is underway against the evils of repression and the need for being oneself. Frequently brushed aside is the question as to what has to be repressed before one can be a self, oneself. The individual potential is first a negative one, a portion of the potential of his society: of aggression, guilt feeling, ignorance, resentment, cruelty which vitiate his life instincts. If the identity of the self is to be more than the immediate realization of this potential (undesirable for the individual as human being), then it requires repression and sublimation, conscious transformation. This process involves at each stage (to use the ridiculed terms which here reveal their succinct concreteness) the negation of the negation, mediation of the immediate, and identity is no more and no less than this process. "Alienation" is the constant and essential element of identity, the objective side of the subject—and not, as it is made to appear today, a disease, a psychological condition. Freud well knew the difference between progressive and regressive, liberating and destructive repression. The publicity of self-actualization promotes the removal of the one and the other, it promotes existence in that immediacy which, in a repressive society, is (to use another Hegelian term) bad immediacy (*schlechte Unmittelbarkeit*). It isolates the individual from the one dimension where he could "find himself": from his political existence, which is at the core of his entire existence. Instead, it encourages nonconformity and letting-go in ways which leave the real engines of repression in the society entirely intact, which even strengthen these engines by substituting the satisfactions of private and personal rebellion for a more than private and personal, and therefore more authentic, opposition. The desublimation involved in this sort of self-actualization is itself repressive inasmuch as it weakens the necessity and the power of the intellect, the catalytic force of that unhappy consciousness which does not revel in the archetypal personal release of frustration—hopeless resurgence of the Id which will sooner or later succumb to the omnipresent rationality of the administered world—but which recognizes the horror of the whole in the most private frustration and actualizes itself in this recognition.

I have tried to show how the changes in advanced democratic societies, which have undermined the basis of economic and political liberalism, have also altered the liberal function of tolerance. The tolerance which was the great achievement of the liberal era is still professed and (with strong qualifications) practiced, while the economic and political process is subjected to an ubiquitous and effective administration in accordance with the predominant interests. The result is an objective contradiction between the economic and political structure on the one side, and the theory and practice of toleration on the other. The altered social structure tends to weaken the effectiveness of tolerance toward dissenting and oppositional movements and to strengthen conservative and reactionary forces. Equality of tolerance becomes abstract, spurious. With the actual decline of dissenting forces in the society, the opposition is insulated in small and frequently antagonistic groups who, even where tolerated within the narrow limits set by the hierarchical structure of society, are powerless while they keep within these limits. But the tolerance shown to them is deceptive and promotes coordination. And on the firm foundations of a coordinated society all but closed against qualitative change, tolerance itself serves to contain such change rather than to promote it.

The same conditions render the critique of such tolerance abstract and academic, and the proposition that the balance between tolerance toward the Right and toward the Left would have to be radically redressed in order to restore the liberating function of tolerance becomes only an unrealistic speculation. Indeed, such a redressing seems to be tantamount to the establishment of a "right of resistance" to the point of subversion. There is not, there cannot be any such right for any group or individual against a constitutional government sustained by a majority of the population. But I believe that there is a "natural right" of resistance for oppressed and overpowered minorities to use extralegal means if the legal ones have proved to be inadequate. Law and order are always and everywhere the law and order which protect the established hierarchy; it is nonsensical to invoke the absolute authority of this law and this order against those who suffer from it and struggle against it—not for personal advantages and revenge, but for their share of humanity. There is no other judge over them than the constituted authorities, the police, and their own conscience. If they use violence, they do not start a new chain of violence but try to break an established one. Since they will be punished, they know the risk, and when they are willing to take it, no third person, and least of all the educator and intellectual, has the right to preach them abstention.

POSTSCRIPT 1968

Under the conditions prevailing in this country, tolerance does not, and cannot, fulfill the civilizing function attributed to it by the liberal protagonist of democracy, namely, protection of dissent. The progressive historical force of tolerance lies in its extension to those modes and forms of dissent which are not committed to the status quo of society and not confined to the institutional framework of the established society. Consequently, the idea of tolerance implies the necessity, for the dissenting group or individuals, to become legitimate if and when the established legitimacy prevents and counteracts the development of dissent. This would be the case not only in a totalitarian society, under a dictatorship, in one-party states, but also in a democracy (representative, parliamentary, or "direct") where the majority does not result from the development of independent thought and opinion but rather from the monopolistic or oligopolistic administration of public opinion, without terror and (normally) without censorship. In such cases, the majority is self-perpetuating while perpetuating the vested interests which *made* it a majority. In its very structure this majority is "closed," petrified; it repels "a priori" any change other than changes within the system. But this means that the majority is no longer justified in claiming the democratic title of the best guardian of the common interest. And such a majority is all but the opposite of Rousseau's "general will": it is composed, not of individuals who, in their political functions, have made effective "abstraction" from their private interests, but, on the contrary, of individuals who have effectively identified their private interests with their political functions. And the representatives of this majority, in ascertaining and executing its will, ascertain and execute the will of the vested interests which have formed the majority. The ideology of democracy hides its lack of substance.

In the United States, this tendency goes hand in hand with the monopolistic or oligopolistic concentration of capital in the formation of public opinion, i.e., of the majority. The chance of influencing, in any effective way, this majority is at a price, in dollars, totally out of reach of the radical opposition. Here too, free competition and exchange of ideas have become a farce. The Left has no equal voice, no equal access to the mass media and their public facilities—not because a conspiracy excludes it, but because, in good old capitalist fashion, it does not have the required purchasing power. And the Left does not have the purchasing power because it is the Left. These conditions impose upon the radical minorities a strategy which is in essence a refusal to allow the continuous functioning of allegedly indiscriminate but in fact discriminate tolerance, for example, a strategy of protesting against the alternate matching of a spokesman for the Right (or Center) with one for the Left. Not "equal" but *more* representation of the Left would be equalization of the prevailing inequality.

Within the solid framework of preestablished inequality and power, tolerance is practiced indeed. Even outrageous opinions are expressed, outrageous incidents are televised; and the critics of established policies are interrupted by the same number of commercials as the conservative advocates. Are these interludes supposed to counteract the sheer weight, magnitude, and continuity of system-publicity, indoctrination which operates playfully through the endless commercials as well as through the entertainment?

Given this situation, I suggested in "Repressive Tolerance" the practice of discriminating tolerance in an inverse direction, as a means of shifting the balance between Right and Left by restraining the liberty of the Right, thus counter-acting the pervasive inequality of freedom (unequal opportunity of access to the means of democratic persuasion) and strengthening the oppressed against the oppressors. Tolerance would be restricted with respect to movements of a demonstrably aggressive or destructive character (destructive of the prospects for peace, justice, and freedom for all). Such discrimination would also be applied to movements opposing the extension of social legislation to the poor, weak, disabled. As against the virulent denunciations that such a policy would do away with the sacred liberalistic principle of equality for "the other side," I maintain that there are issues where either there is no "other side" in any more than a formalistic sense, or where "the other side" is demonstrably "regressive" and impedes possible improvement of the human condition. To tolerate propaganda for inhumanity vitiates the goals not only of liberalism but of every progressive political philosophy.

I presupposed the existence of demonstrable criteria for aggressive, regressive, destructive forces. If the final democratic criterion of the declared opinion of the majority no longer (or rather not yet) prevails, if vital ideas, values, and ends of human progress no longer (or rather not yet) enter, as competing equals, the formation of public opinion, if the people are no longer (or rather not yet) sovereign but "made" by the real sovereign powers—is there any alternative other than the dictatorship of an "elite" over the people? For the opinion of people (usually designated as The People) who are unfree in the very faculties in which liberalism saw the roots of freedom (independent thought and independent speech) can carry no overriding validity and authority—even if The People constitute the overwhelming majority.

If the choice were between genuine democracy and dictatorship, democracy would certainly be preferable. But democracy does not prevail. The radical critics of the existing political process are thus readily denounced as advocating an "elitism," a dictatorship of intellectuals as an alternative. What we have in fact is government, representative government by a nonintellectual minority of politicians, generals, and businessmen. The record of this "elite" is not very promising, and political prerogatives for the intelligentsia may not necessarily be worse for the society as a whole.

In any case, John Stuart Mill, not exactly an enemy of liberal and representative government, was not so allergic to the political leadership of the intelligentsia as the contemporary guardians of semi-democracy are. Mill believed that "individual mental superiority" justifies "reckoning one person's opinion as equivalent to more than one":

> Until there shall have been devised, and until opinion is willing to accept, some mode of plural voting which may assign to education as such the degree of superior influence due to it, and sufficient as a counterpoise to the numerical weight of the least educated class, for so long the benefits of completely universal suffrage cannot be obtained without bringing with them, as it appears to me, more than equivalent evils.[2]

"Distinction in favor of education, right in itself," was also supposed to preserve "the educated from the class legislation of the uneducated," without enabling the former to practice a class legislation of their own.[3]

Today, these words have understandably an anti-democratic, "elitist" sound—understandably because of their dangerously radical implications. For if "education" is more and other than training, learning, preparing for the existing society, it means not only enabling man to know and understand the facts which make up reality but also to know and understand the factors that establish the facts so that he can change their inhuman reality. And such humanistic education would involve the "hard" sciences ("hard" as in the "hardware" bought by the Pentagon?), would free them from their destructive direction. In other words, such education would indeed badly serve the Establishment, and to give political prerogatives to the men and women thus educated would indeed be anti-democratic in the terms of the Establishment. But these are not the only terms.

However, the alternative to the established semi-democratic process is *not* a dictatorship or elite, no matter how intellectual and intelligent, but the struggle for a real democracy. Part of this struggle is the fight against an ideology of tolerance which, in reality, favors and fortifies the conservation of the status quo of inequality and discrimination. For this struggle, I proposed the practice of discriminating tolerance. To be sure, this practice already presupposes the radical goal which it seeks to achieve. I committed this *petitio principii* in order to combat the pernicious ideology that tolerance is already institutionalized in this society. The tolerance which is the life element, the token of a free society, will never be the gift of the powers that be; it can, under the prevailing conditions of tyranny by the majority, only be won in the sustained effort of radical minorities, willing to break this tyranny and to work for the emergence of a free and sovereign majority—minorities intolerant, militantly intolerant and disobedient to the rules of behavior which tolerate destruction and suppression.

NOTES

1. In modern times, fascism has been a consequence of the transition to industrial society *without* a revolution. See Barrington Moore's *Social Origins of Dictatorship and Democracy* (Boston: Beacon Press, 1966).
2. *Considerations on Representative Government* (Chicago: Gateway Edition, 1962), p. 183.
3. *Ibid.*, p. 181.

Index

Accountability, of elites, 22
Agar, Herbert, 90
Agger, Robert, 89, 90, 113
Alexander the Great, 109
Almond, Gabriel A., 26, 60, 68, 110, 114
American political system, challenges to, 49–67
Anti-democratic writers, 93–94
Anton, Thomas J., 91
Apathy, political, 76–78
Aristotle, 94, 96, 109
Aron, Raymond, 10
Authority
  control distinguished from, 17
  crisis of, 3
  elites and, 4–8
  power distinguished from, 2–3

Bachrach, Peter, 1–11, 12, 88, 90
Banfield, Edward, 82, 90
Baratz, Morton, 12, 90–91
Barton, 113
Baudelaire, 144
Bay, Christian, 89

Beer, Samuel, 88, 89, 97
Beloff, Max, 29, 32, 33
Bentham, Jeremy, 28
Berelson, Bernard, 11, 27–48, 88, 89, 97, 102
Bismarck, Otto von, 21
Blumer, Herbert, 89, 91
Bottomore, T. B., 11, 89
Bridgman, Percy W., 25
Bryce, James, 15, 26, 29, 44
Buildings, seizure of, 5
Bureaucracy, 2, 6, 8
Burke, Edmund, 28
Burke, Kenneth, 25
Burnham, James, 110
Burnham, Walter Dean, 90

Calhoun, John, 128
Calvin, John, 25
Campaigns, political, 41
Campbell, Angus, 110, 113
Cardozo, Benjamin, 54
Carnap, R., 25
Centralization, 116, 121–123, 137
Change, 50, 58, 86

China policy, of U.S., in 1940s, 49, 50
Churchill, Winston S., 13
Coalitions, 79
Cobban, Alfred, 28, 48
"Code" of an elite, 24
Coles, Robert, 91
Confrontation, 5
Connolly, William E., 89
Conservatism, 40
Constantini, Edmond, 89
Constitutionalism, 73
Control, authority distinguished from, 17
Converse, Philip E., 90, 110, 114
Copernicus, 119
Corporate elites, 4
Coser, Lewis, 92
Coulton, G. C., 25

Dahl, Robert, 1, 10, 11, 73, 76, 77, 81, 82, 88, 89, 90, 93–109
Dahrendorf, Ralf, 92
Davis, Lane, 89, 101–102
Decentralization
  case for, 116–137
  demands for, 2
Decision-making
  elites and, 1, 4, 5, 6
  general participation in, 69
Democracy
  classical theory of, 69–70, 75, 80, 86
  concept of, 9
  electoral system and, 36–48
  electorate and, 38
  elites and, 10
  elitist theory of, critique of, 69–87, 93–109
  flexibility and, 38–40
  indifference and, 38
  individual and, 29–36
  involvement and, 38
  participatory, 6
  political stability and, 38–40
  in theory and practice, 27–48
Despotism, 55
Dicey, A. V., 26
Dictatorships, 51
Diplomacy, 21
Discussion, political, 30
Dostoevski, Fëdor M., 144
Dublin, Louis I., 114

Duncan, Graeme, 89
Dupeux, Georges, 114

Edison, Thomas, 120
Einstein, Albert, 120
Eiseley, Loren, 129
Eldersveld, Samuel, 89
Electoral system, democracy and, 36–48
Elites
  authority and, 4–8
  concept of, 1, 2, 4, 6, 7, 13–25
  corporate, 4
  decision-making and, 1, 4, 5, 6
  definition of, 2
  democracy and, 10
  established, 8
  new, 8
  perspectives of, 22–23
  political, 1–11, 14, 16–25
  power and, 2–8
  study of, 13–25
Elitism, democratic, 9
Elitist theory of democracy
  critique of, 69–87
  as guide for research, 76–80
  normative implications of, 71–76
  reflections on, 93–109
Essien-Udom, E. V., 90
Established elites, 8

Farganis, James, 89
Federalism, 57
Fisher, Richard, 26
Fishman, Jacob, 90, 91
Flexibility, democracy and, 38–40
Fordham, Jefferson B., 68
Free enterprise system, 4, 121
Freud, Sigmund, 162
Friedrich, Carl, 82, 90

Galbraith, John, 12
Galileo, 119
General Motors, 134
Gerth, Hans, 90
Godts, Father, 15, 113
Goldrich, Daniel, 89
Goldstein, Marshall, 90
Goodman, Paul, 11, 12, 116-137
Government, 17
Greer, Thomas, 91
Grigg, Charles, 88
Gusfield, Joseph, 92
Guttsman, W. L., 26

Hand, Learned, 34–35, 47, 62, 68
Hartz, Louis, 88, 89, 97
Heberle, Rudolf, 84, 91, 107, 114
Hegel, Georg, 8
Higham, John, 92
Hiss affair, 63
Hitler, Adolf, 81
Hobbes, Thomas, 8, 28
Hobsbawn, E. J., 91
Horowitz, Irving Louis, 92
Hull, Clark L., 25

Individual, democracy and, 29–36
Interest, individual, in politics, 30
Interlocking among positions, 19

Jefferson, Thomas, 8, 97, 130
Jennings, M. Kent, 90
Johnson, Lyndon, 3

Kaplan, Abraham, 12, 26
Kariel, Henry, 89
Kaufman, Arnold, 6
Keller, Suzanne, 11
Kelvin, Lord, 119
Key, V. O., 73, 88, 97, 100, 110, 114
Kibbutz, 124
Killian, Lewis, 91
King, Charles, 91
King, Martin Luther, 125
Kirchheimer, Otto, 115
Korzybski, Alfred, 25
Kropotkin, Prince, 119, 124

Lane, Robert, 76, 89, 110
Lang, Gladys, 91
Lang, Karl, 91
Lanternari, Vittorio, 91
Lao-tse, 124
Laski, Harold, 48
Lasswell, Harold D., 2, 4, 10, 12, 13–25, 26, 110
Lazarsfeld, Paul, 27–48, 113
Leaders and leadership, 13, 16, 18, 25, 54, 62, 64, 65, 70, 71–72, 73, 75, 80, 81–86, 93, 94, 96, 125
Le Corbusier (architect), 126
Leites, Nathan, 24, 26
Lenin, V. I., 43, 97
Lerner, Daniel, 12, 13–25
Lincoln, Abraham, 97

Lindblom, Charles, 88, 104, 111–112
Lippmann, Walter, 51–57, 59, 60, 66, 67
Lipset, Seymour Martin, 70, 72, 81, 83, 88, 89, 90, 91, 97, 102, 110, 111, 113
Litt, Edgar, 90
Locke, John, 28, 48
Lohman, J. D., 89
Lorwin, Val R., 115
Lukes, Steven, 89

Machiavelli, 8, 94, 96, 109
MacIver, Robert M., 26, 66, 68
Marcuse, Herbert, 11, 138–168
Marx, Karl, 86, 97
Matthews, Harrison, 128
Mayo, Henry, 88, 97
McCarthy, Joseph, 61-65, 81
McClosky, Herbert, 88–89, 97
McConnell, Grant, 12
McPhee, William, 27–48
Mendel, Gregor, 119
Merriam, Charles E., 26
Michels, Robert, 6, 8, 16, 88, 94, 97, 102, 110
Milbrath, Lester, 73, 88, 89, 90, 97
Mill, John Stuart, 28, 48, 74, 89, 95, 96, 142, 145, 147, 156, 157, 167
Miller, Arthur S., 12, 110
Mills, C. Wright, 12, 56, 68, 89, 90, 97
Moore, Barrington, 169
Morris, Charles W., 25
Morris-Jones, W. H., 89, 97, 111
Mosca, Gaetano, 3, 5, 8, 16, 25, 26, 94, 97
Motivation, for participation in political life, 30

Negroes, 77, 80, 84, 87, 124–125, 126, 129
  suicide rate among, 114
Neubauer, Deane, 113
Neustadt, Richard, 82
New Deal, 129
New elites, 8
Nondecision-making, 6, 7, 8
Nonelites, power and, 5, 6, 7
Northern Student Movement, 132–133

O'Connor, Garrett, 90
Oligarchy, iron law of, 6

Paine, Thomas, 8
Pareto, Vilfredo, 3, 5, 8, 25, 94, 97
Parsons, Talcott, 110
Pasteur, Louis, 119, 120
Peace Corps, 130
Pearl, Stanley, 90
Pennock, J. Roland, 87
Perspectives of elites, 22–23
Philip of Macedon, 109
Philosophy, public, 51–52, 59, 66–67
Plamenatz, John, 10
Plato, 95, 156
Pluralism, in politics, 42
Political elites, 1–11, 14, 16–25
Political system, American, challenges to, 49–67
Political theory, 27–29
Politics, pluralism in, 42
Pollock, Sir Frederick, 26
Polsby, Nelson, 77, 89, 97
Power
    actual, 17
    authority distinguished from, 2–3
    definition of, 16–17
    elites and, 2–8
    nonelites and, 5, 6, 7
    potential, 17
    pyramid of, 24
Presthus, Robert, 89
Prewitt, K., 115
Progressive outlook, 40
Propaganda, 21
Prothro, James, 88
Proudhon, Pierre, 124
Psychology, industrial, 134
Public opinion, 72, 84–85
Public philosophy, 51–52, 59, 66–67

Radical Right, 107
Rationality, voting and, 32
Realists, 9, 11
Reichenbach, Hans, 25
Reitzes, D. C., 89
Representation, 72
Revisionism, 70
Richards, I. A., 25
Robespierre, 154

Roosevelt, Franklin D., 61
Rosenburg, Morris, 90
Rosenhack, S., 115
Ross, J. F., 26
Rothwell, C. Easton, 12, 13–25
Rousseas, Steven W., 89
Rousseau, Jean-Jacques, 8, 94, 96, 111, 130, 165
Rude, George, 91
Rutherford, Ernest, 120

Sabine, George, 87, 92, 97
Saint-Simon, 8, 16, 25, 26
Sanford, Edward, 12
Sartre, Jean Paul, 155
Satori, Giovanni, 10, 11, 12, 110
Schattschneider, E. E., 90
Schlesinger, Arthur M., 26
Schmitt, Carl, 43
Schueller, George K., 26
Schumpeter, Joseph, 9, 10, 27, 32, 71, 82, 88, 97, 110
Searles, Ruth, 91
Self-destruction, danger of, 50–51, 66
Seligman, Ben, 120
Sereno, Renzo, 25, 26
Shils, Edward, 27, 68
Singer, Marshall R., 11
Sit-ins, 5
Smelser, Neil, 91
Smith, Adam, 121
Smith, T. V., 26
Social circulation, 18
Social movements, 84–86, 107–108
    decline in elite power and, 5
Solomon, Frederic, 90, 91
Sorokin, P. A., 26
Sovereignty, 28
"Sputnik" crisis, 49, 50
Stability, political, 38–40
Stalin, Joseph, 20
Stouffer, Samuel A., 64, 68, 88
Stokes, Donald, 89, 110
Supreme Court, U. S., 54, 99
Swanson, Bert, 89, 113

Taine, H. A., 16, 25
Technology, 2, 120, 123, 131
Theory, political, 27–29
Thomson, J. J., 119, 120
Tocqueville, Alexis de, 125
Tolerance, repressive, 138–168

Tolstoy, Leo, 124
Totalitarianism, 51
Truman, David B., 11, 49–67, 73, 88, 97, 100, 110
Tufte, Edward R., 113
Turner, Ralph, 91

United States
  challenges to political system in, 49–67
  China policy of, in 1940s, 49, 50
Urbanization, 128–129, 131

Verba, Sidney, 110, 114

Vesalius, 119

Walker, Jack L., 11, 69–87, 91, 95–109, 110, 111, 113, 114
Walker, Walter L., 90
Waskow, Arthur, 133
Weber, Max, 82, 110
Weimar Republic, 103
Williams, J. Allen, 91
Wilson, James Q., 90
Wind, Edgar, 144
Wolfinger, B. K., 115
Wolfinger, R. E., 115
Wolin, Sheldon, 87